JOHN LAW

(See Page 1)

Extraordinary
Popular Delusions

Charles Mackay

Dover Publications, Inc.
Mineola, New York

Bibliographical Note

This Dover edition, first published in 2003, is an unabridged republication of the work originally published in 1841 by Richard Bentley, London under the title *Memoirs of Extraordinary Popular Delusions*.

Library of Congress Cataloging-in-Publication Data

Mackay, Charles, 1814–1889.
    Extraordinary popular delusions / Charles Mackay.
        p. cm.
    Originally published: London : Richard Bentley, 1841.
    ISBN-13: 978-0-486-43223-6 (pbk.)
    ISBN-10: 0-486-43223-8 (pbk.)
    1. Errors, Popular. 2. Impostors and imposture. 3. Swindlers and swindling. 4. Occultism—Early works to 1900. 5. Delusions. 6. Social psychology. 7. Investments—Psychological aspects. 8. Stock exchanges—Psychological aspects. I. Title.

AZ999.M2 2003
001.9'6—dc21   2003048598

Manufactured in the United States by LSC Communications
43223809   2018
www.doverpublications.com

PREFACE

THE object of the Author in the following pages has been to collect the most remarkable instances of those moral epidemics which have been excited, sometimes by one cause and some-times by another, and to show how easily the masses have been led astray, and how imitative and gregarious men are, even in their infatuations and crimes.

Some of the subjects introduced may be familiar to the reader; but the Author hopes that sufficient novelty of detail will be found even in these, to render them acceptable, while they could not be wholly omitted in justice to the subject of which it was proposed to treat. The memoirs of the South Sea madness and the Mississippi delusion are more complete and copious than are to be found elsewhere; and the same may be said of the history of the Witch Mania, which contains an account of its terrific progress in Germany, a part of the subject which has been left comparatively untouched by Sir Walter Scott, in his "Letters on Demonology and Witchcraft," the most important that have yet appeared on this fearful but most interesting subject.

Popular delusions began so early, spread so widely, and have lasted so long, that instead of two or three volumes, fifty would scarcely suffice to detail their history. The present may be considered more of a miscellany of delusions than a history, —a chapter only in the great and awful book of human folly which yet remains to be written, and which Porson once jestingly said he would write in five hundred volumes! Interspersed are sketches of some lighter matters,—amusing instances of the imitativeness and wrongheadedness of the people, rather than examples of folly and delusion.

Religious manias have been purposely excluded as incompatible with the limits prescribed to the present work;—a mere list of them would alone be sufficient to occupy a volume.

In another volume should these be favourably received, the Author will attempt a complete view of the progress of Alchemy and the philosophical delusions that sprang from it, including the Rosicrucians of a bygone, and the Magnetisers of the present, era.

London, April 23rd, 1841.

CONTENTS

MONEY MANIA.—THE MISSISSIPPI SCHEME

> Some in clandestine companies combine;
> Erect new stocks to trade beyond the line;
> With air and empty names beguile the town,
> And raise new credits first, then cry 'em down;
> Divide the empty nothing into shares,
> And set the crowd together by the ears.—*Defoe.*

THE personal character and career of one man are so intimately connected with the great scheme of the years 1719 and 1720, that a history of the Mississippi madness can have no fitter introduction than a sketch of the life of its great author John Law. Historians are divided in opinion as to whether they should designate him a knave or a madman. Both epithets were unsparingly applied to him in his lifetime, and while the unhappy consequences of his projects were still deeply felt. Posterity, however, has found reason to doubt the justice of the accusation, and to confess that John Law was neither knave nor madman, but one more deceived than deceiving, more sinned against than sinning. He was thoroughly acquainted with the philosophy and true principles of credit. He understood the monetary question better than any man of his day; and if his system fell with a crash so tremendous, it was not so much his fault as that of the people amongst whom he had erected it. He did not calculate upon the avaricious frenzy of a whole nation; he did not see that confidence, like mistrust, could be increased almost *ad infinitum,* and that hope was as extravagant as fear. How was he to foretell that the French people, like the man in the fable, would kill, in their frantic eagerness, the fine goose he had brought to lay them so many golden eggs? His fate was like that which may be supposed to have overtaken the first adventurous boatman who rowed

I

from Erie to Ontario. Broad and smooth was the river on which he embarked; rapid and pleasant was his progress; and who was to stay him in his career? Alas for him! the cataract was nigh. He saw, when it was too late, that the tide which wafted him so joyously along was a tide of destruction; and when he endeavoured to retrace his way, he found that the current was too strong for his weak efforts to stem, and that he drew nearer every instant to the tremendous falls. Down he went over the sharp rocks, and the waters with him. *He* was dashed to pieces with his bark; but the waters, maddened and turned to foam by the rough descent, only boiled and bubbled for a time, and then flowed on again as smoothly as ever. Just so it was with Law and the French people. He was the boatman, and they were the waters.

John Law was born at Edinburgh in the year 1671. His father was the younger son of an ancient family in Fife, and carried on the business of a goldsmith and banker. He amassed considerable wealth in his trade, sufficient to enable him to gratify the wish, so common among his countrymen, of adding a territorial designation to his name. He purchased with this view the estates of Lauriston and Randleston, on the Firth of Forth, on the borders of West and Mid Lothian, and was thenceforth known as Law of Lauriston. The subject of our memoir, being the eldest son, was received into his father's counting-house at the age of fourteen, and for three years laboured hard to acquire an insight into the principles of banking as then carried on in Scotland. He had always manifested great love for the study of numbers, and his proficiency in the mathematics was considered extraordinary in one of his tender years. At the age of seventeen he was tall, strong, and well made; and his face, although deeply scarred with the small-pox, was agreeable in its expression, and full of intelligence. At this time he began to neglect his business, and becoming vain of his person, indulged in considerable extravagance of attire. He was a great favourite with the ladies, by whom he was called Beau Law; while the other sex, despising his foppery, nicknamed him Jessamy John. At the death of his father, which happened in 1688, he withdrew entirely from the desk, which had become so irksome, and being possessed of the revenues of the paternal estate of Lauriston, he proceeded to London, to see the world.

He was now very young, very vain, good-looking, tolerably rich, and quite uncontrolled. It is no wonder that, on his arrival in the capital, he should launch out into extravagance. He soon became a regular frequenter of the gaming-houses, and by pursuing a certain plan, based upon some abstruse calculation of chances, he contrived to gain considerable sums. All the gamblers envied him his luck, and many made it a point to watch his play, and stake their money on the same chances. In affairs of gallantry he was equally fortunate; ladies of the first rank smiled graciously upon the handsome Scotchman—the young, the rich, the witty, and the obliging. But all these successes only paved the way for reverses. After he had been for nine years exposed to the dangerous attractions of the gay life he was leading, he became an irrecoverable gambler. As his love of play increased in violence, it diminished in prudence. Great losses were only to be repaired by still greater ventures, and one unhappy day he lost more than he could repay without mortgaging his family estate. To that step he was driven at last. At the same time his gallantry brought him into trouble. A love affair, or slight flirtation, with a lady of the name of Villiers,* exposed him to the resentment of a Mr. Wilson, by whom he was challenged to fight a duel. Law accepted, and had the ill fortune to shoot his antagonist dead upon the spot. He was arrested the same day, and brought to trial for murder by the relatives of Mr. Wilson. He was afterwards found guilty, and sentenced to death. The sentence was commuted to a fine, upon the ground that the offence only amounted to manslaughter. An appeal being lodged by a brother of the deceased, Law was detained in the King's Bench, whence, by some means or other, which he never explained, he contrived to escape; and an action being instituted against the sheriffs, he was advertised in the Gazette, and a reward offered for his apprehension. He was described as "Captain John Law, a

* Miss Elizabeth Villiers, afterwards Countess of Orkney.

Scotchman, aged twenty-six; a very tall, black, lean man; well shaped, above six feet high, with large pock-holes in his face; big nosed, and speaking broad and loud." As this was rather a caricature than a description of him, it has been supposed that it was drawn up with a view to favour his escape. He succeeded in reaching the Continent, where he travelled for three years, and devoted much of his attention to the monetary and banking affairs of the countries through which he passed. He stayed a few months in Amsterdam, and speculated to some extent in the funds. His mornings were devoted to the study of finance and the principles of trade, and his evenings to the gaming-house. It is generally believed that he returned to Edinburgh in the year 1700. It is certain that he published in that city his *Proposals and Reasons for constituting a Council of Trade*. This pamphlet did not excite much attention.

In a short time afterwards he published a project for establishing what he called a Land-Bank,* the notes issued by which were never to exceed the value of the entire lands of the state, upon ordinary interest, or were to be equal in value to the land, with the right to enter into possession at a certain time. The project excited a good deal of discussion in the Scottish Parliament, and a motion for the establishment of such a bank was brought forward by a neutral party, called the Squadrone, whom Law had interested in his favour. The Parliament ultimately passed a resolution to the effect, that, to establish any kind of paper credit, so as to force it to pass, was an improper expedient for the nation.

Upon the failure of this project, and of his efforts to procure a pardon for the murder of Mr. Wilson, Law withdrew to the Continent, and resumed his old habits of gaming. For fourteen years he continued to roam about, in Flanders, Holland, Germany, Hungary, Italy, and France. He soon became intimately acquainted with the extent of the trade and resources of each, and daily more confirmed in his opinion that no country could prosper without a paper currency. During the whole of this time he appears to have chiefly supported himself by success-

---

* The wits of the day called it a *sand-bank*, which would wreck the vessel of the state.

ful play. At every gambling-house of note in the capitals of Europe he was known and appreciated as one better skilled in the intricacies of chance than any other man of the day. It is stated in the *Biographie Universelle* that he was expelled, first from Venice, and afterwards from Genoa, by the magistrates, who thought him a visitor too dangerous for the youth of those cities. During his residence in Paris he rendered himself obnoxious to D'Argenson, the lieutenant-general of the police, by whom he was ordered to quit the capital. This did not take place, however, before he had made the acquaintance, in the saloons, of the Duke de Vendôme, the Prince de Conti, and of the gay Duke of Orleans, the latter of whom was destined afterwards to exercise so much influence over his fate. The Duke of Orleans was pleased with the vivacity and good sense of the Scottish adventurer, while the latter was no less pleased with the wit and amiability of a prince who promised to become his patron. They were often thrown into each other's society, and Law seized every opportunity to instil his financial doctrines into the mind of one whose proximity to the throne pointed him out as destined, at no very distant date, to play an important part in the government.

Shortly before the death of Louis XIV., or, as some say, in 1780, Law proposed a scheme of finance to Desmarets, the comptroller. Louis is reported to have inquired whether the projector were a Catholic, and on being answered in the negative, to have declined having any thing to do with him.*

It was after this repulse that he visited Italy. His mind being still occupied with schemes of finance, he proposed to Victor Amadeus, Duke of Savoy, to establish his land-bank in that country. The duke replied that his dominions were too circumscribed for the execution of so great a project, and that he was by far too poor a potentate to be ruined. He advised

---

* This anecdote, which is related in the correspondence of Madame de Bavière, Duchess of Orleans and mother of the Regent, is discredited by Lord John Russell in his *History of the principal States of Europe from the Peace of Utrecht;* for what reason he does not inform us. There is no doubt that Law proposed his scheme to Desmarets, and that Louis refused to hear it. The reason given for the refusal is quite consistent with the character of that bigoted and tyrannical monarch.

him, however, to try the king of France once more; for he was
sure, if he knew any thing of the French character, that the
people would be delighted with a plan, not only so new, but so
plausible.

Louis XIV. died in 1715, and the heir to the throne being
an infant only seven years of age, the Duke of Orleans assumed the reins of government, as regent, during his minority.
Law now found himself in a more favourable position. The
tide in his affairs had come, which, taken at the flood, was to
waft him on to fortune. The regent was his friend, already acquainted with his theory and pretensions, and inclined, more-
over, to aid him in any efforts to restore the wounded credit of
France, bowed down to the earth by the extravagance of the
long reign of Louis XIV.

Hardly was that monarch laid in his grave ere the popular
hatred, suppressed so long, burst forth against his memory.
He who, during his life, had been flattered with an excess of
adulation, to which history scarcely offers a parallel, was now
cursed as a tyrant, a bigot, and a plunderer. His statues were
pelted and disfigured; his effigies torn down, amid the execra-
tions of the populace, and his name rendered synonymous with
selfishness and oppression. The glory of his arms was forgotten, and nothing was remembered but his reverses, his extravagance, and his cruelty.

The finances of the country were in a state of the utmost
disorder. A profuse and corrupt monarch, whose profuseness
and corruption were imitated by almost every functionary,
from the highest to the lowest grade, had brought France to the
verge of ruin. The national debt amounted to 3000 millions
of livres, the revenue to 145 millions, and the expenses of government to 142 millions per annum; leaving only three millions
to pay the interest upon 3000 millions. The first care of the
regent was to discover a remedy for an evil of such magnitude,
and a council was early summoned to take the matter into consideration. The Duke de St. Simon was of opinion that nothing
could save the country from revolution but a remedy at once
bold and dangerous. He advised the regent to convoke the
states-general, and declare a national bankruptcy. The Duke

de Noailles, a man of accommodating principles, an accomplished courtier, and totally averse from giving himself any trouble or annoyance that ingenuity could escape from, opposed the project of St. Simon with all his influence. He represented the expedient as alike dishonest and ruinous. The regent was of the same opinion, and this desperate remedy fell to the ground.

The measures ultimately adopted, though they promised fair, only aggravated the evil. The first and most dishonest measure was of no advantage to the state. A recoinage was ordered, by which the currency was depreciated one-fifth; those who took a thousand pieces of gold or silver to the mint received back an amount of coin of the same nominal value, but only four-fifths of the weight of metal. By this contrivance the treasury gained seventy-two millions of livres, and all the commercial operations of the country were disordered. A trifling diminution of the taxes silenced the clamours of the people, and for the slight present advantage the great prospective evil was forgotten.

A Chamber of Justice was next instituted to inquire into the malversations of the loan-contractors and the farmers of the revenues. Tax-collectors are never very popular in any country, but those of France at this period deserved all the odium with which they were loaded. As soon as these farmers-general, with all their hosts of subordinate agents, called *maltôtiers*,* were called to account for their misdeeds, the most extravagant joy took possession of the nation. The Chamber of Justice, instituted chiefly for this purpose, was endowed with very extensive powers. It was composed of the presidents and councils of the parliament, the judges of the Courts of Aid and of Requests, and the officers of the Chamber of Account, under the general presidence of the minister of finance. Informers were encouraged to give evidence against the offenders by the promise of one-fifth part of the fines and confiscations. A tenth of all concealed effects belonging to the guilty was promised to such as should furnish the means of discovering them.

* From *maltôte*, an oppressive tax.

The promulgation of the edict constituting this court caused a degree of consternation among those principally concerned, which can only be accounted for on the supposition that their peculation had been enormous. But they met with no sympathy. The proceedings against them justified their terror. The Bastille was soon unable to contain the prisoners that were sent to it, and the gaols all over the country teemed with guilty or suspected persons. An order was issued to all innkeepers and postmasters to refuse horses to such as endeavoured to seek safety in flight; and all persons were forbidden, under heavy fines, to harbour them or favour their evasion. Some were condemned to the pillory, others to the galleys, and the least guilty to fine and imprisonment. One only, Samuel Bernard, a rich banker and farmer-general of a province remote from the capital, was sentenced to death. So great had been the illegal profits of this man,—looked upon as the tyrant and oppressor of his district,—that he offered six millions of livres, or 250,000*l.* sterling, to be allowed to escape.

His bribe was refused, and he suffered the penalty of death. Others, perhaps more guilty, were more fortunate. Confiscation, owing to the concealment of their treasures by the delinquents, often produced less money than a fine. The severity of the government relaxed, and fines, under the denomination of taxes, were indiscriminately levied upon all offenders; but so corrupt was every department of the administration, that the country benefited but little by the sums which thus flowed into the treasury. Courtiers and courtiers' wives and mistresses came in for the chief share of the spoils. One contractor had been taxed, in proportion to his wealth and guilt, at the sum of twelve millions of livres. The Count * * *, a man of some weight in the government, called upon him, and offered to procure a remission of the fine if he would give him a hundred thousand crowns. "Vous êtes trop tard, mon ami;" replied the financier; "I have already made a bargain with your wife for fifty thousand."*

---

* This anecdote is related by M. de la Hode, in his *Life of Philippe of Orleans*. It would have looked more authentic if he had given the names of the dishonest contractor and the still more dishonest minister. But M.

About a hundred and eighty millions of livres were levied in this manner, of which eighty were applied in payment of the debts contracted by the government. The remainder found its way into the pockets of the courtiers. Madame de Maintenon, writing on this subject, says—"We hear every day of some new grant of the regent. The people murmur very much at this mode of employing the money taken from the peculators." The people, who, after the first burst of their resentment is over, generally express a sympathy for the weak, were indignant that so much severity should be used to so little purpose. They did not see the justice of robbing one set of rogues to fatten another. In a few months all the more guilty had been brought to punishment, and the Chamber of Justice looked for victims in humbler walks of life. Charges of fraud and extortion were brought against tradesmen of good character in consequence of the great inducements held out to common informers. They were compelled to lay open their affairs before this tribunal in order to establish their innocence. The voice of complaint resounded from every side; and at the expiration of a year the government found it advisable to discontinue further proceedings. The Chamber of Justice was suppressed, and a general amnesty granted to all against whom no charges had yet been preferred.

In the midst of this financial confusion Law appeared upon the scene. No man felt more deeply than the regent the deplorable state of the country, but no man could be more averse from putting his shoulders manfully to the wheel. He disliked business; he signed official documents without proper examination, and trusted to others what he should have undertaken himself. The cares inseparable from his high office were burdensome to him. He saw that something was necessary to be done; but he lacked the energy to do it, and had not virtue enough to sacrifice his ease and his pleasures in the attempt. No wonder that, with this character, he listened favourably to

---

de la Hode's book is liable to the same objection as most of the French memoirs of that and of subsequent periods. It is sufficient with most of them that an anecdote be *ben trovato;* the *vero* is but matter of secondary consideration.

the mighty projects, so easy of execution, of the clever adventurer whom he had formerly known, and whose talents he appreciated.

When Law presented himself at court he was most cordially received. He offered two memorials to the regent, in which he set forth the evils that had befallen France, owing to an insufficient currency, at different times depreciated. He asserted that a metallic currency, unaided by a paper money, was wholly inadequate to the wants of a commercial country, and particularly cited the examples of Great Britain and Holland to shew the advantages of paper. He used many sound arguments on the subject of credit, and proposed as a means of restoring that of France, then at so low an ebb among the nations, that he should be allowed to set up a bank, which should have the management of the royal revenues, and issue notes both on that and on landed security. He further proposed that this bank should be administered in the king's name, but subject to the control of commissioners to be named by the States-General.

While these memorials were under consideration, Law translated into French his essay on money and trade, and used every means to extend through the nation his renown as a financier. He soon became talked of. The confidants of the regent spread abroad his praise, and every one expected great things of Monsieur Lass.*

On the 5th of May, 1716, a royal edict was published, by which Law was authorised, in conjunction with his brother, to establish a bank under the name of Law and Company, the notes of which should be received in payment of the taxes. The capital was fixed at six millions of livres, in twelve thousand shares of five hundred livres each, purchasable one fourth in specie, and the remainder in *billets d'état*. It was not thought expedient to grant him the whole of the privileges prayed for in his memorials until experience should have shewn their safety and advantage.

---

* The French pronounced his name in this manner to avoid the ungallic sound, *aw*. After the failure of his scheme, the wags said the nation was *lasse de lui,* and proposed that he should in future be known by the name of Monsieur He*las!*

Law was now on the high road to fortune. The study of thirty years was brought to guide him in the management of his bank. He made all his notes payable at sight, and in the coin current at the time they were issued. This last was a master-stroke of policy, and immediately rendered his notes more valuable than the precious metals. The latter were constantly liable to depreciation by the unwise tampering of the government. A thousand livres of silver might be worth their nominal value one day, and be reduced one-sixth the next, but a note of Law's bank retained its original value. He publicly declared at the same time, that a banker deserved death if he made issues without having sufficient security to answer all demands. The consequence was, that his notes advanced rapidly in public estimation, and were received at one per cent more than specie. It was not long before the trade of the country felt the benefit. Languishing commerce began to lift up her head; the taxes were paid with greater regularity and less murmuring; and a degree of confidence was established that could not fail, if it continued, to become still more advantageous. In the course of a year, Law's notes rose to fifteen per cent premium, while the *billets d'état*, or notes issued by the government as security for the debts contracted by the extravagant Louis XIV., were at a discount of no less than seventy-eight and a half per cent. The comparison was too great in favour of Law not to attract the attention of the whole kingdom, and his credit extended itself day by day. Branches of his bank were almost simultaneously established at Lyons, Rochelle, Tours, Amiens, and Orleans.

The regent appears to have been utterly astonished at his success, and gradually to have conceived the idea that paper, which could so aid a metallic currency, could entirely supersede it. Upon this fundamental error he afterwards acted. In the mean time, Law commenced the famous project which has handed his name down to posterity. He proposed to the regent (who could refuse him nothing) to establish a company that should have the exclusive privilege of trading to the great river Mississippi and the province of Louisiana, on its western bank. The country was supposed to abound in the precious metals; and the company, supported by the profits of their exclusive commerce, were to be the sole farmers of the taxes and sole coiners of money. Letters patent were issued, incorporating the company, in August 1717. The capital was divided into two hundred thousand shares of five hundred livres each, the whole of which might be paid in *billets d'état*, at their nominal value, although worth no more than a hundred and sixty livres in the market.

It was now that the frenzy of speculating began to seize upon the nation. Law's bank had effected so much good, that any promises for the future which he thought proper to make were readily believed. The regent every day conferred new privileges upon the fortunate projector. The bank obtained the monopoly of the sale of tobacco, the sole right of refinage of gold and silver, and was finally erected into the Royal Bank of France. Amid the intoxication of success, both Law and the regent forgot the maxim so loudly proclaimed by the former, that a banker deserved death who made issues of paper without the necessary funds to provide for them. As soon as the bank, from a private, became a public institution, the regent caused a fabrication of notes to the amount of one thousand millions of livres. This was the first departure from sound principles, and one for which Law is not justly blameable. While the affairs of the bank were under his control, the issues had never exceeded sixty millions. Whether Law opposed the inordinate increase is not known; but as it took place as soon as the bank was made a royal establishment, it is but fair to lay the blame on the change of system upon the regent.

Law found that he lived under a despotic government; but he was not yet aware of the pernicious influence which such a government could exercise upon so delicate a framework as that of credit. He discovered it afterwards to his cost, but in the meantime suffered himself to be impelled by the regent into courses which his own reason must have disapproved. With a weakness most culpable, he lent his aid in inundating the country with paper money, which, based upon no solid foundation, was sure to fall, sooner or later. The extraordinary present fortune dazzled his eyes, and prevented him from seeing the evil day that would burst over his head, when once, from any cause or other, the alarm was sounded. The parliament were from the first jealous of his influence as a foreigner, and had, besides, their misgivings as to the safety of his projects. As his influence extended, their animosity increased. D'Aguesseau, the chancellor, was unceremoniously dismissed by the regent for his opposition to the vast increase of paper money, and the constant depreciation of the gold and silver coin of the realm. This only served to augment the enmity of the parliament, and when D'Argenson, a man devoted to the interests of the regent, was appointed to the vacant chancellorship, and made at the same time minister of finance, they became more violent than ever. The first measure of the new minister caused a further depreciation of the coin. In order to extinguish the *billets d'état*, it was ordered that persons bringing to the mint four thousand livres in specie and one thousand livres in *billets d'état*, should receive back coin to the amount of five thousand livres. D'Argenson plumed himself mightily upon thus creating five thousand new and smaller livres out of the four thousand old and larger ones, being too ignorant of the true principles of trade and credit to be aware of the immense injury he was inflicting upon both.

The parliament saw at once the impolicy and danger of such a system, and made repeated remonstrances to the regent. The latter refused to entertain their petitions, when the parliament, by a bold and very unusual stretch of authority, commanded that no money should be received in payment but that of the old standard. The regent summoned a *lit de justice*, and annulled the decree. The parliament resisted, and issued another. Again the regent exercised his privilege, and annulled it, till the parliament, stung to fiercer opposition, passed another decree, dated August 12th, 1718, by which they forbade the bank of Law to have any concern, either direct or indirect, in the administration of the revenue; and prohibited all foreigners, under heavy penalties, from interfering, either in their own names or in that of others, in the management of the finances of the state. The parliament considered Law to be the author of all the evil, and some of the councillors in the virulence of their enmity, proposed that he should be brought to trial, and, if found guilty, be hung at the gates of the Palais de Justice.

Law, in great alarm, fled to the Palais Royal, and threw himself on the protection of the regent, praying that measures might be taken to reduce the parliament to obedience. The regent had nothing so much at heart, both on that account and because of the disputes that had arisen relative to the legitimation of the Duke of Maine and the Count of Thoulouse, the sons of the late king. The parliament was ultimately overawed by the arrest of their president and two of the councillors, who were sent to distant prisons.

Thus the first cloud upon Law's prospects blew over: freed from apprehension of personal danger, he devoted his attention to his famous Mississippi project, the shares of which were rapidly rising, in spite of the parliament. At the commencement of the year 1719, an edict was published, granting to the Mississippi Company the exclusive privilege of trading to the East Indies, China, and the South Seas, and to all the possessions of the French East India Company, established by Colbert. The Company, in consequence of this great increase of their business, assumed, as more appropriate, the title of Company of the Indies, and created fifty thousand new shares. The prospects now held out by Law were most magnificent. He promised a yearly dividend of two hundred livres upon each share of five hundred, which, as the shares were paid for in *billets d'état*, at their nominal value, but worth only 100 livres, was at the rate of about 120 per cent profit.

The public enthusiasm, which had been so long rising, could not resist a vision so splendid. At least three hundred thousand applications were made for the fifty thousand new shares, and Law's house in the Rue de Quincampoix was beset from morning to night by the eager applicants. As it was impossible to satisfy them all, it was several weeks before a list of the fortunate new stockholders could be made out, during which time the public impatience rose to a pitch of frenzy. Dukes, marquises, counts, with their duchesses, marchionesses, and countesses, waited in the streets for hours every day before Mr. Law's door to know the result. At last, to avoid the jostling of the plebeian crowd, which, to the number of thousands, filled the whole thoroughfare, they took apartments in the adjoining houses, that they might be continually near the temple whence the new Plutus was diffusing wealth. Every day the value of the old shares increased, and the fresh applications, induced by the golden dreams of the whole nation, became so numerous that it was deemed advisable to create no less than three hundred thousand new shares, at five thousand livres each, in order that the regent might take advantage of the popular enthusiasm to pay off the national debt. For this purpose, the sum of fifteen hundred millions of livres was necessary. Such was the eagerness of the nation, that thrice the sum would have been subscribed if the government had authorised it.

Law was now at the zenith of his prosperity, and the people were rapidly approaching the zenith of their infatuation. The highest and the lowest classes were alike filled with a vision of boundless wealth. There was not a person of note among the aristocracy, with the exception of the Duke of St. Simon and Marshal Villars, who was not engaged in buying or selling stock. People of every age and sex and condition in life speculated in the rise and fall of the Mississippi bonds. The Rue de Quincampoix was the grand resort of the jobbers, and it being a narrow, inconvenient street, accidents continually occurred in it, from the tremendous pressure of the crowd. Houses in it, worth, in ordinary times, a thousand livres of yearly rent, yielded as much as twelve or sixteen thousand. A cobbler, who had a stall in it, gained about two hundred livres a day by letting it out, and furnishing writing materials to brokers and their clients. The story goes, that a hunchbacked man who stood in the street gained considerable sums by lending his hump as a writing-desk to the eager speculators! The great concourse of persons who assembled to do business brought a still greater concourse of spectators. These again drew all the thieves and immoral characters of Paris to the spot, and constant riots and disturbances took place. At nightfall, it was often found necessary to send a troop of soldiers to clear the street.

Law, finding the inconvenience of his residence, removed

to the Place Vendôme, whither the crowd of *agioteurs* followed him. That spacious square soon became as thronged as the Rue de Quincampoix: from morning to night it presented the appearance of a fair. Booths and tents were erected for the transaction of business and the sale of refreshments, and gamblers with their roulette-tables stationed themselves in the very middle of the place, and reaped a golden, or rather a paper, harvest from the throng. The boulevards and public gardens were forsaken; parties of pleasure took their walks in preference in the Place Vendôme, which became the fashionable lounge of the idle as well as the general rendezvous of the busy. The noise was so great all day, that the chancellor, whose court was situated in the square, complained to the regent and the municipality that he could not hear the advocates. Law, when applied to, expressed his willingness to aid in the removal of the nuisance, and for this purpose entered into a treaty with the Prince de Carignan for the Hôtel de Soissons, which had a garden of several acres in the rear. A bargain was concluded, by which Law became the purchaser of the hotel at an enormous price, the prince reserving to himself the magnificent gardens as a new source of profit. They contained some fine statues and several fountains, and were altogether laid out with much taste. As soon as Law was installed in his new abode, an edict was published, forbidding all persons to buy or sell stock any where but in the gardens of the Hôtel de Soissons. In the midst, among the trees, about five hundred small tents and pavilions were erected, for the convenience of the stock-jobbers. Their various colours, the gay ribands and banners which floated from them, the busy crowds which passed continually in and out—the incessant hum of voices, the noise, the music, and the strange mixture of business and pleasure on the countenances of the throng, all combined to give the place an air of enchantment that quite enraptured the Parisians. The Prince de Carignan made enormous profits while the delusion lasted. Each tent was let at the rate of five hundred livres a month; and, as there were at least five hundred of them, his monthly revenue from this source alone must have amounted to 250,000 livres, or upwards of 10,000*l*. sterling.

The honest old soldier, Marshal Villars, was so vexed to see the folly which had smitten his countrymen, that he never could speak with temper on the subject. Passing one day through the Place Vendôme in his carriage, the choleric gentleman was so annoyed at the infatuation of the people, that he abruptly ordered his coachman to stop, and, putting his head out of the carriage-window, harangued them for full half an hour on their "disgusting avarice." This was not a very wise proceeding on his part. Hisses and shouts of laughter resounded from every side, and jokes without number were aimed at him. There being at last strong symptoms that something more tangible was flying through the air in the direction of his head, the marshal was glad to drive on. He never again repeated the experiment.

Two sober, quiet, and philosophic men of letters, M. de la Motte and the Abbé Terrason, congratulated each other, that they, at least, were free from this strange infatuation. A few days afterward, as the worthy abbé was coming out of the Hôtel de Soissons, whither he had gone to buy shares in the Mississippi, whom should he see but his friend La Motte entering for the same purpose. "Ha!" said the abbé smiling, "is that *you?*" "Yes," said La Motte, pushing past him as fast as he was able; "and can that be *you?*" The next time the two scholars met, they talked of philosophy, of science, and of religion, but neither had courage for a long time to breathe one syllable about the Mississippi. At last, when it was mentioned, they agreed that a man ought never to swear against his doing any one thing, and that there was no sort of extravagance of which even a wise man was not capable.

During this time, Law, the new Plutus, had become all at once the most important personage of the state. The antechambers of the regent were forsaken by the courtiers. Peers, judges, and bishops thronged to the Hôtel de Soissons; officers of the army and navy, ladies of title and fashion, and every one to whom hereditary rank or public employ gave a claim to precedence, were to be found waiting in his ante-chambers to beg for a portion of his India stock. Law was so pestered that he was unable to see one-tenth part of the applicants, and every manœuvre that ingenuity could suggest was employed to gain access to him. Peers, whose dignity would have been outraged if the regent had made them wait half an hour for an interview, were content to wait six hours for the chance of seeing Monsieur Law. Enormous fees were paid to his servants, if they would merely announce their names. Ladies of rank employed the blandishments of their smiles for the same object; but many of them came day after day for a fortnight before they could obtain an audience. When Law accepted an invitation, he was sometimes so surrounded by ladies, all asking to have their names put down in his lists as shareholders in the new stock, that, in spite of his well-known and habitual gallantry, he was obliged to tear himself away *par force*. The most ludicrous stratagems were employed to have an opportunity of speaking to him. One lady, who had striven in vain during several days, gave up in despair all attempts to see him at his own house, but ordered her coachman to keep a strict watch whenever she was out in her carriage, and if he saw Mr. Law coming, to drive against a post and upset her. The coachman promised obedience, and for three days the lady was driven incessantly through the town, praying inwardly for the opportunity to be overturned. At last she espied Mr. Law, and, pulling the string, called out to the coachman, "Upset us now! for God's sake, upset us now!" The coachman drove against a post, the lady screamed, the coach was overturned, and Law, who had seen the *accident*, hastened to the spot to render assistance. The cunning dame was led into the Hôtel de Soissons, where she soon thought it advisable to recover from her fright, and, after apologizing to Mr. Law, confessed her stratagem. Law smiled, and entered the lady in his books as the purchaser of a quantity of India stock. Another story is told of a Madame de Boucha, who, knowing that Mr. Law was at dinner at a certain house, proceeded thither in her carriage, and gave the alarm of fire. The company started from table, and Law among the rest; but seeing one lady making all haste into the house towards him, while everybody else was scampering away, he suspected the trick, and ran off in another direction.

Many other anecdotes are related, which even though they

may be a little exaggerated, are nevertheless worth preserving, as shewing the spirit of that singular period.* The regent was one day mentioning, in the presence of D'Argenson, the Abbé Dubois, and some other persons, that he was desirous of deputing some lady, of the rank at least of a duchess, to attend upon his daughter at Modena: "but," added he, "I do not exactly know where to find one." "No!" replied one, in affected surprise; "I can tell you where to find every duchess in France: you have only to go to Mr. Law's; you will see them every one in his ante-chamber."

M. de Chirac, a celebrated physician, had bought stock at an unlucky period, and was very anxious to sell out. Stock, however, continued to fall for two or three days, much to his alarm. His mind was filled with the subject, when he was suddenly called upon to attend a lady who imagined herself unwell. He arrived, was shewn up stairs, and felt the lady's pulse. "It falls! it falls! good God! it falls continually!" said he musingly, while the lady looked up in his face all anxiety for his opinion. "Oh, M. de Chirac," said she, starting to her feet and ringing the bell for assistance; "I am dying! I am dying! it falls! it falls! it falls!" "What falls?" inquired the doctor in amazement. "My pulse! my pulse!" said the lady; "I must be dying." "Calm your apprehensions, my dear madam," said M. de Chirac; "I was speaking of the stocks. The truth is, I have been a great loser, and my mind is so disturbed, I hardly know what I have been saying."

The price of shares sometimes rose ten or twenty per cent in the course of a few hours, and many persons in the humbler walks of life, who had risen poor in the morning, went to bed in affluence. An extensive holder of stock, being taken ill, sent his servant to sell two hundred and fifty shares, at eight thousand livres each, the price at which they were then quoted. The servant went, and, on his arrival in the Jardin de Soissons,

---

* The curious reader may find an anecdote of the eagerness of the French ladies to retain Law in their company, which will make him blush or smile according as he happens to be very modest or the reverse. It is related in the *Letters of Madame Charlotte Elizabeth de Bavière, Duchess of Orleans*, vol. ii, p. 274.

found that in the interval the price had risen to ten thousand
livres. The difference of two thousand livres on the two hundred
and fifty shares, amounting to 500,000 livres, or 20,000*l.* sterling, he very coolly transferred to his own use, and giving the
remainder to his master, set out the same evening for another
country. Law's coachman in a very short time made money
enough to set up a carriage of his own, and requested permission to leave his service. Law, who esteemed the man, begged
of him as a favour that he would endeavour, before he went, to
find a substitute as good as himself. The coachman consented,
and in the evening brought two of his former comrades, telling
Mr. Law to choose between them, and he would take the other.
Cookmaids and footmen were now and then as lucky, and, in
the full-blown pride of their easily-acquired wealth, made the
most ridiculous mistakes. Preserving the language and manners of their old with the finery of their new station, they
afforded continual subjects for the pity of the sensible, the
contempt of the sober, and the laughter of everybody. But
the folly and meanness of the higher ranks of society were still
more disgusting. One instance alone, related by the Duke de
St. Simon, will shew the unworthy avarice which infected the
whole of society. A man of the name of André, without
character or education, had, by a series of well-timed speculations in Mississippi bonds, gained enormous wealth in an in-
credibly short space of time. As St. Simon expresses it, "he
had amassed mountains of gold." As he became rich, he
grew ashamed of the lowness of his birth, and anxious above all
things to be allied to nobility. He had a daughter, an infant
only three years of age, and he opened a negotiation with the
aristocratic and needy family of D'Oyse, that this child should,
upon certain conditions, marry a member of that house. The
Marquis D'Oyse, to his shame, consented, and promised to
marry her himself on her attaining the age of twelve, if the
father would pay him down the sum of a hundred thousand
crowns, and twenty thousand livres every year until the cele-
bration of the marriage. The Marquis was himself in his thirty-
third year. This scandalous bargain was duly signed and
sealed, the stockjobber furthermore agreeing to settle upon his

daughter, on the marriage-day, a fortune of several millions. The Duke of Brancas, the head of the family, was present throughout the negotiation, and shared in all the profits. St. Simon, who treats the matter with the levity becoming what he thought so good a joke, adds, "that people did not spare their animadversions on this beautiful marriage," and further informs us "that the project fell to the ground some months afterwards by the overthrow of Law, and the ruin of the ambitious Monsieur André." It would appear, however, that the noble family never had the honesty to return the hundred thousand crowns.

Amid events like these, which, humiliating though they be, partake largely of the ludicrous, others occurred of a more serious nature. Robberies in the streets were of daily occurrence, in consequence of the immense sums, in paper, which people carried about with them. Assassinations were also frequent. One case in particular fixed the attention of the whole of France, not only on account of the enormity of the offence, but of the rank and high connexions of the criminal.

The Count d'Horn, a younger brother of the Prince d'Horn, and related to the noble families of D'Aremberg, DeLigne, and DeMontmorency, was a young man of dissipated character, extravagant to a degree, and unprincipled as he was extravagant. In connexion with two other young men as reckless as himself, named Mille, a Piedmontese captain, and one Destampes, or Lestang, a Fleming, he formed a design to rob a very rich broker, who was known, unfortunately for himself, to carry great sums about his person. The count pretended a desire to purchase of him a number of shares in the Company of the Indies, and for that purpose appointed to meet him in a *cabaret*, or low public-house, in the neighbourhood of the Place Vendôme. The unsuspecting broker was punctual to his appointment; so were the Count d'Horn and his two associates, whom he introduced as his particular friends. After a few moments' conversation, the Count d'Horn suddenly sprang upon his victim, and stabbed him three times in the breast with a poniard. The man fell heavily to the ground, and, while the count was employed in rifling his portfolio of bonds in the

Mississippi and Indian schemes to the amount of one hundred thousand crowns, Mille, the Piedmontese, stabbed the unfortunate broker again and again, to make sure of his death. But the broker did not fall without a struggle, and his cries brought the people of the *cabaret* to his assistance. Lestang, the other assassin, who had been set to keep watch at a staircase, sprang from a window and escaped; but Mille and the Count d'Horn were seized in the very act.

This crime, committed in open day, and in so public a place as a *cabaret*, filled Paris with consternation. The trial of the assassins commenced on the following day; and the evidence being so clear, they were both found guilty, and condemned to be broken alive on the wheel. The noble relatives of the Count d'Horn absolutely blocked up the ante-chambers of the regent, praying for mercy on the misguided youth, and alleging that he was insane. The regent avoided them as long as possible, being determined that, in a case so atrocious, justice should take its course. But the importunity of these influential suitors was not to be overcome so silently; and they at last forced themselves into the presence of the regent, and prayed him to save their house the shame of a public execution. They hinted that the Princes d'Horn were allied to the illustrious family of Orleans; and added, that the regent himself would be disgraced if a kinsman of his should die by the hands of a common executioner. The regent, to his credit, was proof against all their solicitations, and replied to their last argument in the words of Corneille:

"Le crime fait la honte, et non pas l'échafaud:"

adding, that whatever shame there might be in the punishment he would very willingly share with the other relatives. Day after day they renewed their entreaties, but always with the same result. At last they thought, that if they could interest the Duke de St. Simon in their favour—a man for whom the regent felt sincere esteem—they might succeed in their object. The duke, a thorough aristocrat, was as shocked as they were that a noble assassin should die by the same death as a plebeian felon, and represented to the regent the impolicy of making enemies of so numerous, wealthy, and powerful a family. He urged, too, that in Germany, where the family of D'Aremberg had large possessions, it was the law, that no relative of a person broken on the wheel could succeed to any public office or employ until a whole generation had passed away. For this reason, he thought the punishment of the guilty might be transmuted into beheading, which was considered all over Europe as much less infamous. The regent was moved by this argument, and was about to consent, when Law, who felt peculiarly interested in the fate of the murdered man, confirmed him in his former resolution to let the law take its course.

The relatives of D'Horn were now reduced to the last extremity. The Prince de Robec Montmorency, despairing of other methods, found means to penetrate into the dungeon of the criminal, and offering him a cup of poison, implored him to save them from disgrace. The Count d'Horn turned away his head, and refused to take it. Montmorency pressed him once more; and losing all patience at his continued refusal, turned on his heel, and exclaiming, "Die, then, as thou wilt, mean-spirited wretch! thou art fit only to perish by the hands of the hangman!" left him to his fate.

D'Horn himself petitioned the regent that he might be beheaded; but Law, who exercised more influence over his mind than any other person, with the exception of the notorious Abbé Dubois, his tutor, insisted that he could not in justice succumb to the self-interested views of the D'Horns. The regent had from the first been of the same opinion: and within six days after the commission of their crime, D'Horn and Mille were broken on the wheel in the Place de Grève. The other assassin, Lestang, was never apprehended.

This prompt and severe justice was highly pleasing to the populace of Paris. Even M. de Quincampoix, as they called Law, came in for a share of their approbation for having induced the regent to show no favour to a patrician. But the number of robberies and assassinations did not diminish; no sympathy was shewn for rich jobbers when they were plundered. The general laxity of public morals, conspicuous enough before, was rendered still more so by its rapid pervasion of the middle classes, who had hitherto remained comparatively pure between the open vices of the class above and the hidden crimes of the class below them. The pernicious love of gambling diffused itself through society, and bore all public and nearly all private virtue before it.

For a time, while confidence lasted, an impetus was given to trade which could not fail to be beneficial. In Paris especially the good results were felt. Strangers flocked into the capital from every part, bent not only upon making money, but on spending it. The Duchess of Orleans, mother of the regent, computes the increase of the population during this time, from the great influx of strangers from all parts of the world, at 305,000 souls. The housekeepers were obliged to make up beds in garrets, kitchens, and even stables, for the accommodation of lodgers; and the town was so full of carriages and vehicles of every description, that they were obliged, in the principal streets, to drive at a foot-pace for fear of accidents. The looms of the country worked with unusual activity to supply rich laces, silks, broad-cloth, and velvets, which being paid for in abundant paper, increased in price fourfold. Provisions shared the general advance. Bread, meat, and vegetables were sold at prices greater than had ever before been known; while the wages of labour rose in exactly the same proportion. The artisan who formerly gained fifteen sous per diem now gained sixty. New houses were built in every direction; an illusory prosperity shone over the land, and so dazzled the eyes of the whole nation, that none could see the dark cloud on the horizon announcing the storm that was too rapidly approaching.

Law himself, the magician whose wand had wrought so surprising a change, shared, of course, in the general prosperity. His wife and daughter were courted by the highest nobility, and their alliance sought by the heirs of ducal and princely houses. He bought two splendid estates in different parts of France, and entered into a negotiation with the family of the Duke de Sully for the purchase of the marquisate of Rosny. His religion being an obstacle to his advancement, the regent promised, if he would publicly conform to the Catholic faith, to make him comptroller-general of the finances. Law, who had no more real religion than any other professed gambler, readily agreed, and was confirmed by the Abbé de Tencin in the cathedral of Melun, in presence of a great crowd of spectators.* On the following day he was elected honorary churchwarden of the parish of St. Roch, upon which occasion he made it a present of the sum of five hundred thousand livres. His charities, always magnificent, were not always so ostentatious. He gave away great sums privately, and no tale of real distress ever reached his ears in vain.

At this time he was by far the most influential person of the state. The Duke of Orleans had so much confidence in his sagacity and the success of his plans, that he always consulted him upon every matter of moment. He was by no means unduly elevated by his prosperity, but remained the same simple, affable, sensible man that he had shewn himself in adversity. His gallantry, which was always delightful to the fair objects of it, was of a nature so kind, so gentlemanly, and so respectful, that not even a lover could have taken offence at it. If upon any occasion he showed any symptoms of haughtiness, it was to the cringing nobles who lavished their adulation upon him till it became fulsome. He often took pleasure in seeing how long he could make them dance attendance upon him for a single favour. To such of his own countrymen as by chance visited Paris, and sought an interview with him, he was, on the contrary, all politeness and attention. When Archibald Campbell, Earl of Islay, and afterwards Duke of Argyle, called upon him in the Place Vendôme, he had to pass through an ante-

---

* The following squib was circulated on the occasion:
> "Foin de ton zèle séraphique,
> Malheureux Abbé de Tencin,
> Depuis que Law est Catholique,
> Tout le royaume est Capucin!"

Thus somewhat weakly and paraphrastically rendered by Justandsond, in his translation of the *Memoirs of Louis XV.*:
> "Tencin, a curse on thy seraphic zeal,
> Which by persuasion hath contrived the means
> To make the Scotchman at our altars kneel,
> Since which we all are poor as Capucines!"

chamber crowded with persons of the first distinction, all anxious to see the great financier, and have their names put down as first on the list of some new subscription. Law himself was quietly sitting in his library, writing a letter to the gardener at his paternal estate of Lauriston, about the planting of some cabbages! The earl stayed a considerable time, played a game of piquet with his countryman, and left him charmed with his ease, good sense, and good breeding.

Among the nobles who, by means of the public credulity at this time, gained sums sufficient to repair their ruined fortunes, may be mentioned the names of the Dukes de Bourbon, de Guiche, de la Force,* de Chaulnes, and d'Antin; the Maréchal d'Estrées; the Princes de Rohan, de Poix, and de Léon. The Duke de Bourbon, son of Louis XIV. by Madame de Montespan, was peculiarly fortunate in his speculations in Mississippi paper. He rebuilt the royal residence of Chantilly in a style of unwonted magnificence; and being passionately fond of horses, he erected a range of stables, which were long renowned throughout Europe, and imported a hundred and fifty of the finest racers from England to improve the breed in France. He bought a large extent of country in Picardy, and became possessed of nearly all the valuable lands lying between the Oise and the Somme.

When fortunes such as these were gained, it is no wonder that Law should have been almost worshipped by the mercurial population. Never was monarch more flattered than he was. All the small poets and *littérateurs* of the day poured floods of adulation upon him. According to them, he was the saviour of the country, the tutelary divinity of France; wit was in all his words, goodness in all his looks, and wisdom in all his actions. So great a crowd followed his carriage whenever he went abroad, that the regent sent him a troop of horse as his permanent escort to clear the streets before him.

* The Duke de la Force gained considerable sums, not only by jobbing in the stocks but in dealing in porcelain, spices, &c. It was debated for a length of time in the parliament of Paris whether he had not, in his quality of spice-merchant, forfeited his rank in the peerage. It was decided in the negative. A caricature of him was made, dressed as a street-porter, carrying a large bale of spices on his back, with the inscription, "Admirez La Force."

It was remarked at this time that Paris had never before been so full of objects of elegance and luxury. Statues, pictures, and tapestries were imported in great quantities from foreign countries, and found a ready market. All those pretty trifles in the way of furniture and ornament which the French excel in manufacturing were no longer the exclusive playthings of the aristocracy, but were to be found in abundance in the houses of traders and the middle classes in general. Jewellery of the most costly description was brought to Paris as the most favourable mart; among the rest, the famous diamond bought by the regent, and called by his name, and which long adorned the crown of France. It was purchased for the sum of two millions of livres, under circumstances which shew that the regent was not so great a gainer as some of his subjects by the impetus which trade had received. When the diamond was first offered to him, he refused to buy it, although he desired above all things to possess it, alleging as his reason, that his duty to the country he governed would not allow him to spend so large a sum of the public money for a mere jewel. This valid and honourable excuse threw all the ladies of the court into alarm, and nothing was heard for some days but expressions of regret that so rare a gem should be allowed to go out of France, no private individual being rich enough to buy it. The regent was continually importuned about it, but all in vain, until the Duke de St. Simon, who with all his ability, was something of a twaddler, undertook the weighty business. His entreaties being seconded by Law, the good-natured regent gave his consent, leaving to Law's ingenuity to find the means to pay for it. The owner took security for the payment of the sum of two millions of livres within a stated period, receiving in the mean time the interest of five per cent upon that amount, and being allowed, besides, all the valuable clippings of the gem. St. Simon, in his *Memoirs,* relates with no little complacency his share in this transaction. After describing the diamond to be as large as a greengage, of a form nearly round, perfectly white, and without flaw, and weighing more than five hundred grains, he concludes with a chuckle, by telling the world "that he takes great credit to himself for having induced the regent to make so illustrious a purchase." In other words, he was proud that he had induced him to sacrifice his duty, and buy a bauble for himself at an extravagant price out of the public money.

Thus the system continued to flourish till the commencement of the year 1720. The warnings of the Parliament, that too great a creation of paper money would, sooner or later, bring the country to bankruptcy, were disregarded. The regent, who knew nothing whatever of the philosophy of finance, thought that a system which had produced such good effects could never be carried to excess. If five hundred millions of paper had been of such advantage, five hundred millions additional would be of still greater advantage. This was the grand error of the regent, and which Law did not attempt to dispel. The extraordinary avidity of the people kept up the delusion; and the higher the price of Indian and Mississippi stock, the more *billets de banque* were issued to keep pace with it. The edifice thus reared might not unaptly be compared to the gorgeous palace erected by Potemkin, that princely barbarian of Russia, to surprise and please his imperial mistress: huge blocks of ice were piled one upon another; Ionic pillars of chastest workmanship, in ice, formed a noble portico; and a dome of the same material, shone in the sun, which had just strength enough to gild, but not to melt it. It glittered afar, like a palace of crystals and diamonds; but there came one warm breeze from the south, and the stately building dissolved away, till none were able even to gather up the fragments. So with Law and his paper system. No sooner did the breath of popular mistrust blow steadily upon it, than it fell to ruins, and none could raise it up again.

The first slight alarm that was occasioned was early in 1720. The Prince de Conti, offended that Law should have denied him fresh shares in India stock, at his own price, sent to his bank to demand payment in specie of so enormous a quantity of notes, that three waggons were required for its transport. Law complained to the regent, and urged on his attention the mischief that would be done, if such an example found many imitators. The regent was but too well aware of it, and, sending for the

Prince de Conti, ordered him, under penalty of his high displeasure, to refund to the bank two-thirds of the specie which he had withdrawn from it. The prince was forced to obey the despotic mandate. Happily for Law's credit, De Conti was an unpopular man: everybody condemned his meanness and cupidity, and agreed that Law had been hardly treated. It is strange, however, that so narrow an escape should not have made both Law and the regent more anxious to restrict their issues. Others were soon found who imitated from motives of distrust, the example which had been set by De Conti in revenge. The more acute stockjobbers imagined justly that prices could not continue to rise for ever. Bourdon and La Richardière, renowned for their extensive operations in the funds, quietly and in small quantities at a time, converted their notes into specie, and sent it away to foreign countries. They also bought as much as they could conveniently carry of plate and expensive jewellery, and sent it secretly away to England or to Holland. Vermalet, a jobber, who sniffed the coming storm, procured gold and silver coin to the amount of nearly a million of livres, which he packed in a farmer's cart, and covered over with hay and cow-dung. He then disguised himself in the dirty smock-frock, or *blouse*, of a peasant, and drove his precious load in safety into Belgium. From thence he soon found means to transport it to Amsterdam.

Hitherto no difficulty had been experienced by any class in procuring specie for their wants. But this system could not long be carried on without causing a scarcity. The voice of complaint was heard on every side, and inquiries being instituted, the cause was soon discovered. The council debated long on the remedies to be taken, and Law, being called on for his advice, was of opinion, that an edict should be published, depreciating the value of coin five per cent below that of paper. The edict was published accordingly; but failing of its intended effect, was followed by another, in which the depreciation was increased to ten per cent. The payments of the bank were at the same time restricted to one hundred livres in gold, and ten in silver. All these measures were nugatory to restore confidence in the paper, though the restriction of cash payments within limits so extremely narrow kept up the credit of the bank.

Notwithstanding every effort to the contrary, the precious metals continued to be conveyed to England and Holland. The little coin that was left in the country was carefully treasured, or hidden until the scarcity became so great, that the operations of trade could no longer be carried on. In this emergency, Law hazarded the bold experiment of forbidding the use of specie altogether. In February 1720 an edict was published, which, instead of restoring the credit of the paper, as was intended, destroyed it irrecoverably, and drove the country to the very brink of revolution. By this famous edict it was forbidden to any person whatever to have more than five hundred livres (20*l.*) of coin in his possession, under pain of a heavy fine, and confiscation of the sums found. It was also forbidden to buy up jewellery, plate, and precious stones, and informers were encouraged to make search for offenders, by the promise of one-half the amount they might discover. The whole country sent up a cry of distress at this unheard-of tyranny. The most odious persecution daily took place. The privacy of families was violated by the intrusion of informers and their agents. The most virtuous and honest were denounced for the crime of having been seen with a *louis d'or* in their possession. Servants betrayed their masters, one citizen became a spy upon his neighbour, and arrests and confiscations so multiplied, that the courts found a difficulty in getting through the immense increase of business thus occasioned. It was sufficient for an informer to say that he suspected any person of concealing money in his house, and immediately a search-warrant was granted. Lord Stair, the English ambassador, said, that it was now impossible to doubt of the sincerity of Law's conversion to the Catholic religion; he had established the *inquisition*, after having given abundant evidence of his faith in *transubstantiation*, by turning so much gold into paper.

Every epithet that popular hatred could suggest was showered upon the regent and the unhappy Law. Coin, to any amount above five hundred livres, was an illegal tender, and nobody would take paper if he could help it. No one knew to-day what his notes would be worth to-morrow. "Never," says

Duclos, in his *Secret Memoirs of the Regency,* "was seen a more capricious government—never was a more frantic tyranny exercised by hands less firm. It is inconceivable to those who were witnesses of the horrors of those times, and who look back upon them now as on a dream, that a sudden revolution did not break out—that Law and the regent did not perish by a tragical death. They were both held in horror, but the people confined themselves to complaints; a sombre and timid despair, a stupid consternation, had seized upon all, and men's minds were too vile even to be capable of a courageous crime." It would appear that, at one time, a movement of the people was organised. Seditious writings were posted up against the walls, and were sent, in hand-bills, to the houses of the most conspicuous people. One of them, given in the *Mémoires de la Régence,* was to the following effect:—"Sir and madam,—This is to give you notice that a St. Bartholomew's Day will be enacted again on Saturday and Sunday, if affairs do not alter. You are desired not to stir out, nor you, nor your servants. God preserve you from the flames! Give notice to your neighbours. Dated, Saturday, May 25th, 1720." The immense number of spies with which the city was infested rendered the people mistrustful of one another, and beyond some trifling disturbances made in the evening by an insignificant group, which was soon dispersed, the peace of the capital was not compromised.

The value of shares in the Louisiana, or Mississippi stock, had fallen very rapidly, and few indeed were found to believe the tales that had once been told of the immense wealth of that region. A last effort was therefore tried to restore the public confidence in the Mississippi project. For this purpose, a general conscription of all the poor wretches in Paris was made by order of government. Upwards of six thousand of the very refuse of the population were impressed, as if in time of war, and were provided with clothes and tools to be embarked for New Orleans, to work in the gold mines alleged to abound there. They were paraded day after day through the streets with their pikes and shovels, and then sent off in small detachments to the out-ports to be shipped for America. Two-thirds of them never reached their destination, but dispersed themselves over the country, sold their tools for what they could get, and returned to their old course of life. In less than three weeks afterwards, one-half of them were to be found again in Paris. The manœuvre, however, caused a trifling advance in Mississippi stock. Many persons of superabundant gullibility believed that operations had begun in earnest in the new Golconda, and that gold and silvet ingots would again be found in France.

In a constitutional monarchy some surer means would have been found for the restoration of public credit. In England, at a subsequent period, when a similar delusion had brought on similar distress, how different were the measures taken to repair the evil! but in France, unfortunately, the remedy was left to the authors of the mischief. The arbitrary will of the regent, which endeavoured to extricate the country, only plunged it deeper into the mire. All payments were ordered to be made in paper, and between the 1st of February and the end of May, notes were fabricated to the amount of upwards of 1500 millions of livres, or 60,000,000l. sterling. But the alarm once sounded, no art could make the people feel the slightest confidence in paper which was not exchangeable into metal. M. Lambert, the president of the parliament of Paris, told the regent to his face that he would rather have a hundred thousand livres in gold or silver than five millions in the notes of his bank. When such was the general feeling, the superabundant issues of paper but increased the evil, by rendering still more enormous the disparity between the amount of specie and notes in circulation. Coin, which it was the object of the regent to depreciate, rose in value on every fresh attempt to diminish it. In February, it was judged advisable that the Royal Bank should be incorporated with the Company of the Indies. An edict to that effect was published and registered by the parliament. The state remained the guarantee for the notes of the bank, and no more were to be issued without an order in council. All the profits of the bank, since the time it had been taken out of Law's hands and made a national institution, were given over by the regent to the Company of the Indies. This measure had the effect of raising for a short time the value of the

Louisiana and other shares of the company, but it failed in placing public credit on any permanent basis.

A council of state was held in the beginning of May, at which Law, D'Argenson (his colleague in the administration of the finances), and all the ministers were present. It was then computed that the total amount of notes in circulation was 2600 millions of livres, while the coin in the country was not quite equal to half that amount. It was evident to the majority of the council that some plan must be adopted to equalize the currency. Some proposed that the notes should be reduced to the value of the specie, while others proposed that the nominal value of the specie should be raised till it was on an equality with the paper. Law is said to have opposed both these projects, but failing in suggesting any other, it was agreed that the notes should be depreciated one half. On the 21st of May, an edict was accordingly issued, by which it was decreed that the shares of the Company of the Indies, and the notes of the bank, should gradually diminish in value, till at the end of a year they should only pass current for one-half of their nominal worth. The parliament refused to register the edict—the greatest outcry was excited, and the state of the country became so alarming, that, as the only means of preserving tranquillity, the council of the regency was obliged to stultify its own proceedings, by publishing within seven days another edict, restoring the notes to their original value.

On the same day (the 27th of May) the bank stopped payment in specie. Law and D'Argenson were both dismissed from the ministry. The weak, vacillating, and cowardly regent threw the blame of all the mischief upon Law, who, upon presenting himself at the Palais Royal, was refused admittance. At nightfall, however, he was sent for, and admitted into the palace by a secret door,* when the regent endeavoured to console him, and made all manner of excuses for the severity with which in public he had been compelled to treat him. So capricious was his conduct, that, two days afterwards, he took him publicly to the opera, where he sat in the royal box alongside of

* Duclos, *Mémoires Secrets de la Régence.*

the regent, who treated him with marked consideration in face of all the people. But such was the hatred against Law that the experiment had well nigh proved fatal to him. The mob assailed his carriage with stones just as he was entering his own door; and if the coachman had not made a sudden jerk into the court-yard, and the domestics closed the gate immediately, he would, in all probability, have been dragged out and torn to pieces. On the following day, his wife and daughter were also assailed by the mob as they were returning in their carriage from the races. When the regent was informed of these occurrences he sent Law a strong detachment of Swiss guards, who were stationed night and day in the court of his residence. The public indignation at last increased so much, that Law, finding his own house, even with this guard, insecure, took refuge in the Palais Royal, in the apartments of the regent.

The Chancellor, D'Aguesseau, who had been dismissed in 1718 for his opposition to the projects of Law, was now recalled to aid in the restoration of credit. The regent acknowledged too late, that he had treated with unjustifiable harshness and mistrust one of the ablest, and perhaps the sole honest public man of that corrupt period. He had retired ever since his disgrace to his country house at Fresnes, where, in the midst of severe but delightful philosophic studies, he had forgotten the intrigues of an unworthy court. Law himself, and the Chevalier de Conflans, a gentleman of the regent's household, were despatched in a post-chaise with orders to bring the ex-chancellor to Paris along with them. D'Aguesseau consented to render what assistance he could, contrary to the advice of his friends, who did not approve that he should accept any recall to office of which Law was the bearer. On his arrival in Paris, five councillors of the parliament were admitted to confer with the Commissary of Finance; and on the 1st of June an order was published abolishing the law which made it criminal to amass coin to the amount of more than five hundred livres. Every one was permitted to have as much specie as he pleased. In order that the bank-notes might be withdrawn, twenty-five millions of new notes were created, on the security of the revenues of the city of Paris, at two and a half per cent. The bank-notes withdrawn were publicly burned in front of the Hôtel de Ville. The new notes were principally of the value of ten livres each; and on the 10th of June the bank was re-opened, with a sufficiency of silver coin to give in change for them.

These measures were productive of considerable advantage. All the population of Paris hastened to the bank to get coin for their small notes; and silver becoming scarce, they were paid in copper. Very few complained that this was too heavy, although poor fellows might be continually seen toiling and sweating along the streets, laden with more than they could comfortably carry, in the shape of change for fifty livres. The crowds around the bank were so great that hardly a day passed that some one was not pressed to death. On the 9th of July, the multitude was so dense and clamorous that the guards stationed at the entrance of the Mazarin Gardens closed the gate and refused to admit any more. The crowd became incensed, and flung stones through the railings upon the soldiers. The latter, incensed in their turn, threatened to fire upon the people. At that instant one of them was hit by a stone, and, taking up his piece, he fired into the crowd. One man fell dead immediately, and another was severely wounded. It was every instant expected that a general attack would have been commenced upon the bank; but the gates of the Mazarin Gardens being opened to the crowd, who saw a whole troop of soldiers, with their bayonets fixed ready to receive them, they contented themselves by giving vent to their indignation in groans and hisses.

Eight days afterwards the concourse of people was so tremendous that fifteen persons were squeezed to death at the doors of the bank. The people were so indignant that they took three of the bodies on stretchers before them, and proceeded, to the number of seven or eight thousand, to the gardens of the Palais Royal, that they might show the regent the misfortunes that he and Law had brought upon the country. Law's coachman, who was sitting on the box of his master's carriage, in the court-yard of the palace, happened to have more zeal than discretion, and, not liking that the mob should abuse his master, he said, loud enough to be overheard by several persons, that they were all blackguards, and deserved to be hanged. The mob immediately set upon him, and thinking that Law was in the carriage, broke it to pieces. The imprudent coachman narrowly escaped with his life. No further mischief was done; a body of troops making their appearance, the crowd quietly dispersed, after an assurance had been given by the regent that the three bodies they had brought to shew him should be decently buried at his own expense. The parliament was sitting at the time of this uproar, and the president took upon himself to go out and see what was the matter. On his return he informed the councillors that Law's carriage had been broken by the mob. All the members rose simultaneously, and expressed their joy by a loud shout, while one man, more zealous in his hatred than the rest, exclaimed, "*And Law himself, is* he *torn to pieces?*"*

Much, undoubtedly, depended on the credit of the Company of the Indies, which was answerable for so great a sum to the nation. It was therefore suggested in the council of the ministry, that any privileges which could be granted to enable it to fulfil its engagements, would be productive of the best results. With this end in view, it was proposed that the exclusive privilege of all maritime commerce should be secured to it, and an edict to that effect was published. But it was unfortunately forgotten that by such a measure all the merchants of the country would be ruined. The idea of such an immense privilege was generally scouted by the nation, and petition on petition was presented to the parliament that they would refuse to register the decree. They refused accordingly, and the regent, remarking that they did nothing but fan the flame of sedition, exiled them to Blois. At the intercession of D'Aguesseau, the place

---

*The Duchess of Orleans gives a different version of this story; but whichever be the true one, the manifestation of such feeling in a legislative assembly was not very creditable. She says that the president was so transported with joy, that he was seized with a rhyming fit, and returning into the hall, exclaimed to the members:

"*Messieurs! Messieurs! bonne nouvelle!*
Le carrosse de Lass est reduit en cannelle!"

of banishment was changed to Pontoise, and thither accordingly the councillors repaired, determined to set the regent at defiance. They made every arrangement for rendering their temporary exile as agreeable as possible. The president gave the most elegant suppers, to which he invited all the gayest and wittiest company of Paris. Every night there was a concert and ball for the ladies. The usually grave and solemn judges and councillors joined in cards and other diversions, leading for several weeks a life of the most extravagant pleasure, for no other purpose than to show the regent of how little consequence they deemed their banishment, and that, when they willed it, they could make Pontoise a pleasanter residence than Paris.

Of all the nations in the world the French are the most renowned for singing over their grievances. Of that country it has been remarked with some truth, that its whole history may be traced in its songs. When Law, by the utter failure of his best-laid plans, rendered himself obnoxious, satire of course seized hold upon him; and while caricatures of his person appeared in all the shops, the streets resounded with songs, in which neither he nor the regent was spared. Many of these songs were far from decent; and one of them in particular counselled the application of all his notes to the most ignoble use to which paper can be applied. But the following, preserved in the letters of the Duchess of Orleans, was the best and the most popular, and was to be heard for months in all the *carrefours* in Paris. The application of the chorus is happy enough:

> Aussitôt que Lass arriva
> Dans notre bonne ville,
> Monsieur le Régent publia
> Que Lass serait utile
> Pour rétablir la nation.
> *La faridondaine! la faridondon!*
> Mais il nous a tous enrichi,
> *Biribi!*
> *A la façon de Barbari,*
> *Mon ami*

> Ce parpaillot, pour attirer
>   Tout l'argent de la France,
> Songea d'abord à s'assurer
>   De notre confiance.
> Il fit son abjuration,
> *La faridondaine! la faridondon!*
> Mais le fourbe s'est converti,
>   *Biribi!*
> *A la façon de Barbari,*
>   *Mon ami!*
>
> Lass, le fils aîné de Satan
>   Nous met tous à l'aumône,
> Il nous a pris tout notre argent
>   Et n'en rend à personne.
> Mais le Régent, humain et bon,
> *La faridondaine! la faridondon!*
> Nous rendra ce qu'on nous a pris,
>   *Biribi!*
> *A la façon de Barbari,*
>   *Mon ami!*

The following epigram is of the same date:

> *Lundi*, j'achetai des actions;
> *Mardi*, je gagnai des millions;
> *Mercredi*, j'arrangeai mon ménage,
> *Jeudi*, je pris un équipage,
> *Vendredi*, je m'en fus au bal,
> *Et Samedi*, à l'hôpital.

Among the caricatures that were abundantly published, and that shewed as plainly as graver matters that the nation had awakened to a sense of its folly, was one, a fac-simile of which is preserved in the *Mémoires de la Régence*. It was thus described by its author: "The 'Goddess of Shares,' in her triumphal car, driven by the Goddess of Folly. Those who are drawing the car are impersonations of the Mississippi, with his wooden leg, the South Sea, the Bank of England, the Company of the West of Senegal, and of various assurances. Lest the car should not roll fast enough, the agents of these companies, known by their long fox-tails and their cunning looks, turn round the spokes of the wheels, upon which are marked the names of the several stocks and their value, sometimes high and sometimes low, according to the turns of the wheel. Upon the ground are the merchandise, day-books and ledgers of legitimate commerce, crushed under the chariot of Folly. Behind is an immense crowd of persons, of all ages, sexes, and conditions, clamouring after Fortune, and fighting with each other to get a portion of the shares which she distributes so bountifully among them. In the clouds sits a demon, blowing bubbles of soap, which are also the objects of the admiration and cupidity of the crowd, who jump upon one another's backs to reach them ere they burst. Right in the pathway of the car, and blocking up the passage, stands a large building, with three doors, through one of which it must pass, if it proceeds farther, and all the crowd along with it. Over the first door are the words, '*Hôpital des Foux,*' over the second, '*Hôpital des Malades,*' and over the third, '*Hôpital des Gueux.*'" Another caricature represented Law sitting in a large cauldron, boiling over the flames of popular madness, surrounded by an impetuous multitude, who were pouring all their gold and silver into it, and receiving gladly in exchange the bits of paper which he distributed among them by handfuls.

While this excitement lasted, Law took good care not to expose himself unguarded in the streets. Shut up in the apartments of the regent, he was secure from all attack; and whenever he ventured abroad, it was either *incognito,* or in one of the royal carriages, with a powerful escort. An amusing anecdote is recorded of the detestation in which he was held by the people, and the ill-treatment he would have met had he fallen into their hands. A gentleman of the name of Boursel was passing in his carriage down the Rue St. Antoine, when his farther progress was stayed by a hackney-coach that had blocked up the road. M. Boursel's servant called impatiently to the hackney-coachman to get out of the way, and, on his refusal, struck him a blow on the face. A crowd was soon drawn together by the disturbance, and M. Boursel got out of the carriage to restore order. The hackney-coachman, imagining that he had now another assailant, bethought him of an expedient to rid himself of both, and called out as loudly as he was able, "Help! help! murder! murder! Here are Law and his servant going to kill me! Help! help!" At this cry the people came out of their shops, armed with sticks and other weapons, while the mob gathered stones to inflict summary vengeance upon the supposed financier. Happily for M. Boursel and his servant, the door of the church of the Jesuits stood wide open, and, seeing the fearful odds against them, they rushed towards it with all speed. They reached the altar, pursued by the people, and would have been ill-treated even there if, finding the door open leading to the sacristy, they had not sprang through, and closed it after them. The mob were then persuaded to leave the church by the alarmed and indignant priests, and finding M. Boursel's carriage still in the streets, they vented their ill-will against it, and did it considerable damage.

The twenty-five millions secured on the municipal revenues of the city of Paris, bearing so low an interest as two and a half per cent, were not very popular among the large holders of Mississippi stock. The conversion of the securities was, therefore, a work of considerable difficulty; for many preferred to retain the falling paper of Law's company, in the hope that a favourable turn might take place. On the 15th of August, with a view to hasten the conversion, an edict was passed, declaring that all notes for sums between one thousand and ten thousand livres should not pass current, except for the purchase of annuities and bank accounts, or for the payment of instalments still due on the shares of the company.

In October following another edict was passed, depriving these notes of all value whatever after the month of November next ensuing. The management of the mint, the farming of the revenue, and all the other advantages and privileges of the India, or Mississippi Company, were taken from them, and they were reduced to a mere private company. This was the death-blow to the whole system, which had now got into the hands of its enemies. Law had lost all influence in the Council of Finance, and the company, being despoiled of its immunities, could no longer hold out the shadow of a prospect of being able to fulfil its engagements. All those suspected of illegal profits at the time the public delusion was at its height, were sought out and amerced in heavy fines. It was previously ordered that a list of the original proprietors should be made out, and that such persons as still retained their shares should place them in deposit with the company, and that those who had neglected to complete the shares for which they had put down their names should now purchase them of the company, at the rate of 13,500 livres for each share of 500 livres. Rather than submit to pay this enormous sum for stock which was actually at a discount, the shareholders packed up all their portable effects, and endeavoured to find a refuge in foreign countries. Orders were immediately issued to the authorities at the ports and frontiers, to apprehend all travellers who sought to leave the kingdom, and keep them in custody, until it was ascertained whether they had any plate or jewellery with them, or were concerned in the late stock-jobbing. Against such few as escaped, the punishment of death was recorded, while the most arbitrary proceedings were instituted against those who remained.

Law himself, in a moment of despair, determined to leave a country where his life was no longer secure. He at first only demanded permission to retire from Paris to one of his country-seats—a permission which the regent cheerfully granted. The latter was much affected at the unhappy turn affairs had taken, but his faith continued unmoved in the truth and efficacy of Law's financial system. His eyes were opened to his own errors; and during the few remaining years of his life he constantly longed for an opportunity of again establishing the system upon a securer basis. At Law's last interview with the prince, he is reported to have said,—"I confess that I have committed many faults. I committed them because I am a man, and all men are liable to error; but I declare to you most solemnly that none of them proceeded from wicked or dishonest motives, and that nothing of the kind will be found in the whole course of my conduct."

Two or three days after his departure the regent sent him a very kind letter, permitting him to leave the kingdom whenever he pleased, and stating that he had ordered his passports to be made ready. He at the same time offered him any sum of money he might require. Law respectfully declined the money, and set out for Brussels in a post-chaise belonging to Madame de Prie, the mistress of the Duke of Bourbon, escorted by six horse-guards. From thence he proceeded to Venice, where he remained for some months, the object of the greatest curiosity to the people, who believed him to be the possessor of enormous wealth. No opinion, however, could be more erroneous. With more generosity than could have been expected from a man who during the greatest part of his life had been a professed gambler, he had refused to enrich himself at the expense of a ruined nation. During the height of the popular frenzy for Mississippi stock, he had never doubted of the final success of his projects in making France the richest and most powerful nation of Europe. He invested all his gains in the purchase of landed property in France—a sure proof of his own belief in the stability of his schemes. He had hoarded no plate or jewellery, and sent no money, like the dishonest jobbers, to foreign countries. His all, with the exception of one diamond, worth about five or six thousand pounds sterling, was invested in the French soil; and when he left that country, he left it almost a beggar. This fact alone ought to rescue his memory from the charge of knavery, so often and so unjustly brought against him.

As soon as his departure was known, all his estates and his valuable library were confiscated. Among the rest, an annuity of 200,000 livres (8000l. sterling) on the lives of his wife and children, which had been purchased for five millions of livres, was forfeited, notwithstanding that a special edict, drawn up for the purpose in the days of his prosperity, had expressly declared that it should never be confiscated for any cause whatever. Great discontent existed among the people that Law had been suffered to escape. The mob and the parliament would have been pleased to have seen him hanged. The few who had not suffered by the commercial revolution re-

LAW IN A CAR DRAWN BY COCKS

joiced that the *quack* had left the country; but all those (and they were by far the most numerous class) whose fortunes were implicated regretted that his intimate knowledge of the distress of the country, and of the causes that had led to it, had not been rendered more available in discovering a remedy.

At a meeting of the Council of Finance and the General Council of the Regency, documents were laid upon the table, from which it appeared that the amount of notes in circulation was 2700 millions. The regent was called upon to explain how it happened that there was a discrepancy between the dates at which these issues were made and those of the edicts by which they were authorised. He might have safely taken the whole blame upon himself, but he preferred that an absent man should bear a share of it; and he therefore stated that Law, upon his own authority, had issued 1200 millions of notes at different times, and that he (the regent), seeing that the thing had been irrevocably done, had screened Law by antedating the decrees of the council which authorised the augmentation. It would have been more to his credit if he had told the whole truth while he was about it, and acknowledged that it was mainly through his extravagance and impatience that Law had been induced to overstep the bounds of safe speculation. It was also ascertained that the national debt, on the 1st of January, 1721, amounted to upwards of 3100 millions of livres, or more than 124,000,000*l.* sterling, the interest upon which was 3,196,000*l.* A commission, or *visa*, was forthwith appointed to examine into all the securities of the state creditors, who were to be divided into five classes; the first four comprising those who had purchased their securities with real effects, and the latter comprising those who could give no proofs that the transactions they had entered into were real and *bonâ fide*. The securities of the latter were ordered to be destroyed, while those of the first four classes were subjected to a most rigid and jealous scrutiny. The result of the labours of the *visa* was a report, in which they counselled the reduction of the interest upon these securities to fifty-six millions of livres. They justified this advice by a statement of the various acts of peculation and extortion which they had discovered; and an edict to that effect was accordingly published and duly registered by the parliaments of the kingdom.

Another tribunal was afterwards established under the title of the *Chambre de l'Arsenal,* which took cognisance of all the malversations committed in the financial departments of the government during the late unhappy period. A Master of Requests, named Falhonet, together with the Abbé Clement, and two clerks in their employ, had been concerned in divers acts of peculation to the amount of upwards of a million of livres. The first two were sentenced to be beheaded, and the latter to be hanged; but their punishment was afterwards commuted into imprisonment for life in the Bastille. Numerous other acts of dishonesty were discovered, and punished by fine and imprisonment.

D'Argenson shared with Law and the regent the unpopularity which had alighted upon all those concerned in the Mississippi madness. He was dismissed from his post of Chancellor to make room for D'Aguesseau; but he retained the title of Keeper of Seals, and was allowed to attend the councils whenever he pleased. He thought it better, however, to withdraw from Paris, and live for a time a life of seclusion at his country seat. But he was not formed for retirement; and becoming moody and discontented, he aggravated a disease under which he had long laboured, and died in less than a twelve-month. The populace of Paris so detested him, that they carried their hatred even to his grave. As his funeral procession passed to the church of St. Nicholas du Chardonneret, the burying-place of his family, it was beset by a riotous mob; and his two sons, who were following as chief mourners, were obliged to drive as fast as they were able down a by-street to escape personal violence.

As regards Law, he for some time entertained a hope that he should be recalled to France to aid in establishing its credit upon a firmer basis. The death of the regent in 1723, who expired suddenly as he was sitting by the fireside conversing with his mistress, the Duchess de Phalaris, deprived him of that hope, and he was reduced to lead his former life of gambling. He was more than once obliged to pawn his diamond, the sole remnant of his vast wealth, but successful play generally enabled him to redeem it. Being persecuted by his creditors at Rome, he proceeded to Copenhagen, where he received permission from the English ministry to reside in his native country, his pardon for the murder of Mr. Wilson having been sent over to him in 1719. He was brought over in the admiral's ship—a circumstance which gave occasion for a short debate in the House of Lords. Earl Coningsby complained that a man who had renounced both his country and his religion should have been treated with such honour, and expressed his belief that his presence in England, at a time when the people were so bewildered by the nefarious practices of the South-Sea directors, would be attended with no little danger. He gave notice of a motion on the subject; but it was allowed to drop, no other member of the House having the slightest participation in his lordship's fears. Law remained for about four years in England, and then proceeded to Venice, where he died in 1729, in very embarrassed circumstances. The following epitaph was written at the time:

> "Ci gît cet Ecossais célébre,
> Ce calculateur sans égal,
> Qui, par les régles de l'algébre,
> A mis la France à l'hôpital."

His brother, William Law, who had been concerned with him in the administration both of the bank and the Louisiana Company, was imprisoned in the Bastille for alleged malversation, but no guilt was ever proved against him. He was liberated after fifteen months, and became the founder of a family, which is still known in France under the title of Marquises of Lauriston.

In the next chapter will be found an account of the madness which infected the people of England at the same time, and under very similar circumstances, but which, thanks to the energies and good sense of a constitutional government, was attended with results far less disastrous than those which were seen in France.

THE SOUTH-SEA BUBBLE

At length corruption, like a general flood,
Did deluge all; and avarice creeping on,
Spread, like a low-born mist, and hid the sun.
Statesmen and patriots plied alike the stocks,
Peeress and butler shared alike the box;
And judges jobbed, and bishops bit the town,
And mighty dukes packed cards for half-a-crown:
Britain was sunk in lucre's sordid charms.—*Pope*.

THE South-Sea Company was originated by the celebrated
Harley Earl of Oxford, in the year 1711, with the view of
restoring public credit, which had suffered by the dismissal
of the Whig ministry, and of providing for the discharge of
the army and navy debentures, and other parts of the floating
debt, amounting to nearly ten millions sterling. A company
of merchants, at that time without a name, took this debt
upon themselves, and the government agreed to secure them
for a certain period the interest of six per cent. To provide
for this interest, amounting to 600,000*l*. per annum, the duties
upon wines, vinegar, India goods, wrought silks, tobacco,
whale-fins, and some other articles, were rendered permanent.
The monopoly of the trade to the South Seas was granted,
and the company, being incorporated by act of parliament,
assumed the title by which it has ever since been known.
The minister took great credit to himself for his share in this
transaction, and the scheme was always called by his flatterers
"the Earl of Oxford's masterpiece."

Even at this early period of its history the most visionary
ideas were formed by the company and the public of the
immense riches of the eastern coast of South America. Every
body had heard of the gold and silver mines of Peru and

Mexico; every one believed them to be inexhaustible, and that it was only necessary to send the manufactures of England to the coast to be repaid a hundredfold in gold and silver ingots by the natives. A report industriously spread, that Spain was willing to concede four ports on the coasts of Chili and Peru for the purposes of traffic, increased the general confidence, and for many years the South-Sea Company's stock was in high favour.

Philip V. of Spain, however, never had any intention of admitting the English to a free trade in the ports of Spanish America. Negotiations were set on foot, but their only result was the *assiento* contract, or the privilege of supplying the colonies with negroes for thirty years, and of sending once a year a vessel, limited both as to tonnage and value of cargo, to trade with Mexico, Peru, or Chili. The latter permission was only granted upon the hard condition, that the King of Spain should enjoy one-fourth of the profits, and a tax of five per cent on the remainder. This was a great disappointment to the Earl of Oxford and his party, who were reminded much oftener than they found agreeable of the

"Parturiunt montes, nascitur ridiculus mus."

But the public confidence in the South-Sea Company was not shaken. The Earl of Oxford declared that Spain would permit two ships, in addition to the annual ship, to carry out merchandise during the first year; and a list was published, in which all the ports and harbours of these coasts were pompously set forth as open to the trade of Great Britain. The first voyage of the annual ship was not made till the year 1717, and in the following year the trade was suppressed by the rupture with Spain.

The king's speech, at the opening of the session of 1717, made pointed allusion to the state of public credit, and recommended that proper measures should be taken to reduce the national debt. The two great monetary corporations, the South-Sea Company and the Bank of England, made proposals to parliament on the 20th of May ensuing. The South-

Sea Company prayed that their capital stock of ten millions might be increased to twelve, by subscription or otherwise, and offered to accept five per cent instead of six upon the whole amount. The bank made proposals equally advantageous. The house debated for some time, and finally three acts were passed, called the South-Sea Act, the Bank Act, and the General Fund Act. By the first, the proposals of the South-Sea Company were accepted, and that body held itself ready to advance the sum of two millions towards discharging the principal and interest of the debt due by the state for the four lottery funds of the ninth and tenth years of Queen Anne. By the second act, the bank received a lower rate of interest for the sum of 1,775,027*l.* 15*s.* due to it by the state, and agreed to deliver up to be cancelled as many exchequer bills as amounted to two millions sterling, and to accept of an annuity of one hundred thousand pounds, being after the rate of five per cent, the whole redeemable at one year's notice. They were further required to be ready to advance, in case of need, a sum not exceeding 2,500,000*l.* upon the same terms of five per cent interest, redeemable by parliament. The General Fund Act recited the various deficiencies, which were to be made good by the aids derived from the foregoing sources.

The name of the South-Sea Company was thus continually before the public. Though their trade with the South American States produced little or no augmentation of their revenues, they continued to flourish as a monetary corporation. Their stock was in high request, and the directors, buoyed up with success, began to think of new means for extending their influence. The Mississippi scheme of John Law, which so dazzled and captivated the French people, inspired them with an idea that they could carry on the same game in England. The anticipated failure of his plans did not divert them from their intention. Wise in their own conceit, they imagined they could avoid his faults, carry on their schemes for ever, and stretch the cord of credit to its extremest tension, without causing it to snap asunder.

It was while Law's plan was at its greatest height of popularity, while people were crowding in thousands to the Rue Quincampoix, and ruining themselves with frantic eagerness, that the South-Sea directors laid before parliament their famous plan for paying off the national debt. Visions of boundless wealth floated before the fascinated eyes of the people in the two most celebrated countries of Europe. The English commenced their career of extravagance somewhat later than the French; but as soon as the delirium seized them, they were determined not to be outdone. Upon the 22d of January, 1720, the House of Commons resolved itself into a committee of the whole house, to take into consideration that part of the king's speech at the opening of the session which related to the public debts, and the proposal of the South-Sea Company towards the redemption and sinking of the same. The proposal set forth at great length, and under several heads, the debts of the state, amounting to 30,981,-712l., which the company were anxious to take upon themselves, upon consideration of five per cent per annum, secured to them until Midsummer 1727; after which time, the whole was to become redeemable at the pleasure of the legislature, and the interest to be reduced to four per cent. The proposal was received with great favour; but the Bank of England had many friends in the House of Commons, who were desirous that that body should share in the advantages that were likely to accrue. On behalf of this corporation it was represented, that they had performed great and eminent services to the state in the most difficult times, and deserved, at least, that if any advantage was to be made by public bargains of this nature, they should be preferred before a company that had never done any thing for the nation. The further consideration of the matter was accordingly postponed for five days. In the mean time a plan was drawn up by the governors of the bank. The South-Sea Company, afraid that the bank might offer still more advantageous terms to the government than themselves, reconsidered their former proposal, and made some alterations in it, which they hoped would render it more acceptable. The principal change was a stipulation that the government might redeem these debts at the expira-

tion of four years, instead of seven, as at first suggested. The
bank resolved not to be outbidden in this singular auction,
and the governors also reconsidered their first proposal, and
sent in a new one.

Thus, each corporation having made two proposals, the
house began to deliberate. Mr. Robert Walpole was the
chief speaker in favour of the bank, and Mr. Aislabie, the
Chancellor of the Exchequer, the principal advocate on behalf
of the South-Sea Company. It was resolved, on the 2d of
February, that the proposals of the latter were most advantageous to the country. They were accordingly received, and
leave was given to bring in a bill to that effect.

Exchange Alley was in a fever of excitement. The company's stock, which had been at a hundred and thirty the
previous day, gradually rose to three hundred, and continued
to rise with the most astonishing rapidity during the whole
time that the bill in its several stages was under discussion.
Mr. Walpole was almost the only statesman in the House
who spoke out boldly against it. He warned them, in eloquent and solemn language, of the evils that would ensue.
It countenanced, he said, "the dangerous practice of stock-
jobbing, and would divert the genius of the nation from trade
and industry. It would hold out a dangerous lure to decoy the
unwary to their ruin, by making them part with the earnings
of their labour for a prospect of imaginary wealth. The great
principle of the project was an evil of first-rate magnitude; it
was to raise artificially the value of the stock, by exciting and
keeping up a general infatuation, and by promising dividends
out of funds which could never be adequate to the purpose."
In a prophetic spirit he added, that if the plan succeeded, the
directors would become masters of the government, form a
new and absolute aristocracy in the kingdom, and control the
resolutions of the legislature. If it failed, which he was convinced it would, the result would bring general discontent and
ruin upon the country. Such would be the delusion, that when
the evil day came, as come it would, the people would start
up, as from a dream, and ask themselves if these things
could have been true. All his eloquence was in vain. He

was looked upon as a false prophet, or compared to the hoarse raven, croaking omens of evil. His friends, however, compared him to Cassandra, predicting evils which would only be believed when they come home to men's hearths, and stared them in the face at their own boards. Although, in former times, the House had listened with the utmost attention to every word that fell from his lips, the benches became deserted when it was known that he would speak on the South-Sea question.

The bill was two months in its progress through the House of Commons. During this time every exertion was made by the directors and their friends, and more especially by the chairman, the noted Sir John Blunt, to raise the price of the stock. The most extravagant rumours were in circulation. Treaties between England and Spain were spoken of, whereby the latter was to grant a free trade to all her colonies; and the rich produce of the mines of Potosi-la-Paz was to be brought to England until silver should become almost as plentiful as iron. For cotton and woollen goods, with which we could supply them in abundance, the dwellers in Mexico were to empty their golden mines. The company of merchants trading to the South Seas would be the richest the world ever saw, and every hundred pounds invested in it would produce hundreds per annum to the stockholder. At last the stock was raised by these means to near four hundred; but, after fluctuating a good deal, settled at three hundred and thirty, at which price it remained when the bill passed the Commons by a majority of 172 against 55.

In the House of Lords the bill was hurried through all its stages with unexampled rapidity. On the 4th of April it was read a first time; on the 5th, it was read a second time; on the 6th, it was committed; and on the 7th, was read a third time and passed.

Several peers spoke warmly against the scheme; but their warnings fell upon dull, cold ears. A speculating frenzy had seized them as well as the plebeians. Lord North and Grey said the bill was unjust in its nature, and might prove fatal in its consequences, being calculated to enrich the few and impoverish the many. The Duke of Wharton followed; but, as he only retailed at second-hand the arguments só eloquently stated by Walpole in the Lower House, he was not listened to with even the same attention that had been bestowed upon Lord North and Grey. Earl Cowper followed on the same side, and compared the bill to the famous horse of the siege of Troy. Like that, it was ushered in and received with great pomp and acclamations of joy, but bore within it treachery and destruction. The Earl of Sunderland endeavoured to answer all objections; and on the question being put, there appeared only seventeen peers against, and eighty-three in favour of the project. The very same day on which it passed the Lords, it received the royal assent, and became the law of the land.

It seemed at that time as if the whole nation had turned stock-jobbers. Exchange Alley was every day blocked up by crowds, and Cornhill was impassable for the number of carriages. Every body came to purchase stock. "Every fool aspired to be a knave." In the words of a ballad published at the time, and sung about the streets,*

> "Then stars and garters did appear
>   Among the meaner rabble;
> To buy and sell, to see and hear
>   The Jews and Gentiles squabble.
>
> The greatest ladies thither came,
>   And plied in chariots daily,
> Or pawned their jewels for a sum
>   To venture in the Alley."

The inordinate thirst of gain that had afflicted all ranks of society was not to be slaked even in the South Sea. Other schemes, of the most extravagant kind, were started. The share-lists were speedily filled up, and an enormous traffic carried on in shares, while, of course, every means were re-

* A *South-Sea Ballad; or, Merry Remarks upon Exchange-Alley Bubbles. To a new Tune called "The Grand Elixir; or, the Philosopher's Stone discovered."*

sorted to to raise them to an artificial value in the market.

Contrary to all expectations, South-Sea stock fell when the bill received the royal assent. On the 7th of April the shares were quoted at three hundred and ten, and on the following day at two hundred and ninety. Already the directors had tasted the profits of their scheme, and it was not likely that they should quietly allow the stock to find its natural level without an effort to raise it. Immediately their busy emissaries were set to work. Every person interested in the success of the project endeavoured to draw a knot of listeners around him, to whom he expatiated on the treasures of the South American seas. Exchange Alley was crowded with attentive groups. One rumour alone, asserted with the utmost confidence, had an immediate effect upon the stock. It was said that Earl Stanhope had received overtures in France from the Spanish government to exchange Gibraltar and Port Mahon for some places on the coast of Peru, for the security and enlargement of the trade in the South Seas. Instead of one annual ship trading to those ports, and allowing the king of Spain twenty-five per cent out of the profits, the company might build and charter as many ships as they pleased, and pay no per centage whatever to any foreign potentate.

"Visions of ingots danced before their eyes,"

and stock rose rapidly. On the 12th of April, five days after the bill had become law, the directors opened their books for a subscription of a million, at the rate of 300*l*. for every 100*l*. capital. Such was the concourse of persons of all ranks, that this first subscription was found to amount to above two millions of original stock. It was to be paid at five payments, of 60*l*. each for every 100*l*. In a few days the stock advanced to three hundred and forty, and the subscriptions were sold for double the price of the first payment. To raise the stock still higher, it was declared, in a general court of directors, on the 21st of April, that the midsummer dividend should be ten per cent, and that all subscriptions should be entitled to the same. These resolutions answering the end designed, the directors, to improve the infatuation of the monied men, opened their books for a second subscription of a million, at four hundred per cent. Such was the frantic eagerness of people of every class to speculate in these funds, that in the course of a few hours no less than a million and a half was subscribed at that rate.

In the mean time, innumerable joint-stock companies started up every where. They soon received the name of Bubbles, the most appropriate that imagination could devise. The populace are often most happy in the nicknames they employ. None could be more apt than that of Bubbles. Some of them lasted for a week or a fortnight, and were no more heard of, while others could not even live out that short span of existence. Every evening produced new schemes, and every morning new projects. The highest of the aristocracy were as eager in this hot pursuit of gain as the most plodding jobber in Cornhill. The Prince of Wales became governor of one company, and is said to have cleared 40,000*l.* by his speculations.* The Duke of Bridgewater started a scheme for the improvement of London and Westminster, and the Duke of Chandos another. There were nearly a hundred different projects, each more extravagant and deceptive than the other. To use the words of the *Political State,* they were "set on foot and promoted by crafty knaves, then pursued by multitudes of covetous fools, and at last appeared to be, in effect, what their vulgar appellation denoted them to be—bubbles and mere cheats." It was computed that near one million and a half sterling was won and lost by these unwarrantable practices, to the impoverishment of many a fool, and the enriching of many a rogue.

Some of these schemes were plausible enough, and, had they been undertaken at a time when the public mind was unexcited, might have been pursued with advantage to all concerned. But they were established merely with the view of raising the shares in the market. The projectors took the first opportunity of a rise to sell out, and next morning the scheme

---

* Coxe's *Walpole,* Correspondence between Mr. Secretary Craggs and Earl Stanhope.

was at an end. Maitland, in his *History of London*, gravely informs us, that one of the projects which received great encouragement, was for the establishment of a company "to make deal boards out of saw-dust." This is no doubt intended as a joke; but there is abundance of evidence to shew that dozens of schemes, hardly a whit more reasonable, lived their little day, ruining hundreds ere they fell. One of them was for a wheel for perpetual motion—capital one million; another was "for encouraging the breed of horses in England, and improving of glebe and church lands, and repairing and rebuilding parsonage and vicarage houses." Why the clergy, who were so mainly interested in the latter clause, should have taken so much interest in the first, is only to be explained on the supposition that the scheme was projected by a knot of the fox-hunting parsons, once so common in England. The shares of this company were rapidly subscribed for. But the most absurd and preposterous of all, and which shewed, more completely than any other, the utter madness of the people, was one started by an unknown adventurer, entitled, *"A company for carrying on an undertaking of great advantage, but nobody to know what it is."* Were not the fact stated by scores of credible witnesses, it would be impossible to believe that any person could have been duped by such a project. The man of genius who essayed this bold and successful inroad upon public credulity, merely stated in his prospectus that the required capital was half a million, in five thousand shares of 100*l*. each, deposit 2*l*. per share. Each subscriber, paying his deposit, would be entitled to 100*l*. per annum per share. How this immense profit was to be obtained, he did not condescend to inform them at that time, but promised that in a month full particulars should be duly announced, and a call made for the remaining 98*l*. of the subscription. Next morning, at nine o'clock, this great man opened an office in Cornhill. Crowds of people beset his door, and when he shut up at three o'clock, he found that no less than one thousand shares had been subscribed for, and the deposits paid. He was thus, in five hours, the winner of 2000*l*. He was philosopher enough to be contented with his venture, and set off the same evening for the Continent. He was never heard of again.

Well might Swift exclaim, comparing Change Alley to a gulf in the South Sea:

> "Subscribers here by thousands float,
>   And jostle one another down,
> Each paddling in his leaky boat,
>   And here they fish for gold and drown.
>
> Now buried in the depths below,
>   Now mounted up to heaven again,
> They reel and stagger to and fro,
>   At their wits' end, like drunken men.
>
> Meantime, secure on Garraway cliffs,
>   A savage race, by shipwrecks fed,
> Lie waiting for the foundered skiffs,
>   And strip the bodies of the dead."

Another fraud that was very successful was that of the "Globe *Permits*," as they were called. They were nothing more than square pieces of playing-cards, on which was the impression of a seal, in wax, bearing the sign of the Globe Tavern, in the neighbourhood of Exchange Alley, with the inscription of "Sail-Cloth Permits." The possessors enjoyed no other advantage from them than permission to subscribe at some future time to a new sail-cloth manufactory, projected by one who was then known to be a man of fortune, but who was afterwards involved in the peculation and punishment of the South-Sea directors. These permits sold for as much as sixty guineas in the Alley.

Persons of distinction, of both sexes, were deeply engaged in all these bubbles; those of the male sex going to taverns and coffee-houses to meet their brokers, and the ladies resorting for the same purpose to the shops of milliners and haberdashers. But it did not follow that all these people believed in the feasibility of the schemes to which they subscribed; it was enough for their purpose that their shares would, by stock-

jobbing arts, be soon raised to a premium, when they got rid
of them with all expedition to the really credulous. So great
was the confusion of the crowd in the alley, that shares in the
same bubble were known to have been sold at the same instant
ten per cent higher at one end of the alley than at the other.
Sensible men beheld the extraordinary infatuation of the people with sorrow and alarm. There were some both in and out
of parliament who foresaw clearly the ruin that was impend-
ing. Mr. Walpole did not cease his gloomy forebodings. His
fears were shared by all the thinking few, and impressed most
forcibly upon the government. On the 11th of June, the day
the parliament rose, the king published a proclamation, declaring that all these unlawful projects should be deemed public nuisances, and prosecuted accordingly, and forbidding any
broker, under a penalty of five hundred pounds, from buying
or selling any shares in them. Notwithstanding this proclamation, roguish speculators still carried them on, and the deluded
people still encouraged them. On the 12th of July, an order
of the Lords Justices assembled in privy council was published, dismissing all the petitions that had been presented for
patents and charters, and dissolving all the bubble companies.
The following copy of their lordships' order, containing a list
of all these nefarious projects, will not be deemed uninteresting at the present time, when, at periodic intervals, there is
but too much tendency in the public mind to indulge in similar practices:

"At the Council Chamber, Whitehall, the 12th day of
    July, 1720. Present, their Excellencies the Lords
    Justices in Council.

"Their Excellencies the Lords Justices, in council, taking
into consideration the many inconveniences arising to the public from several projects set on foot for raising of joint-stock
for various purposes, and that a great many of his majesty's
subjects have been drawn in to part with their money on pre-
tence of assurances that their petitions for patents and charters to enable them to carry on the same would be granted:

to prevent such impositions, their excellencies this day ordered the said several petitions, together with such reports from the Board of Trade, and from his majesty's attorney and solicitor-general, as had been obtained thereon, to be laid before them; and after mature consideration thereof, were pleased, by advice of his majesty's privy council, to order that the said petitions be dismissed, which are as follow:

"1. Petition of several persons, praying letters patent for carrying on a fishing trade by the name of the Grand Fishery of Great Britain.

"2. Petition of the Company of the Royal Fishery of England, praying letters patent for such further powers as will effectually contribute to carry on the said fishery.

"Petition of George James, on behalf of himself and divers persons of distinction concerned in a national fishery, praying letters patent of incorporation, to enable them to carry on the same.

"4. Petition of several merchants, traders, and others, whose names are thereunto subscribed, praying to be incorporated for reviving and carrying on a whale fishery to Greenland and elsewhere.

"5. Petition of Sir John Lambert and others thereto subscribing, on behalf of themselves and a great number of merchants, praying to be incorporated for carrying on a Greenland trade, and particularly a whale fishery in Davis's Straits.

"6. Another petition for a Greenland trade.

"7. Petition of several merchants, gentlemen, and citizens, praying to be incorporated for buying and building of ships to let or freight.

"8. Petition of Samuel Antrim and others, praying for letters patent for sowing hemp and flax.

"9. Petition of several merchants, masters of ships, sail-makers, and manufacturers of sail-cloth, praying a charter of incorporation, to enable them to carry on and promote the said manufactory by a joint-stock.

"10. Petition of Thomas Boyd and several hundred merchants, owners and masters of ships, sail-makers, weavers, and other traders, praying a charter of incorporation, empowering them to borrow money for purchasing lands, in order to the manufacturing sail-cloth and fine holland.

"11. Petition on behalf of several persons interested in a patent granted by the late King William and Queen Mary for the making of linen and sail-cloth, praying that no charter may be granted to any persons whatsoever for making sail-cloth, but that the privilege now enjoyed by them may be confirmed, and likewise an additional power to carry on the cotton and cotton-silk manufactures.

"12. Petition of several citizens, merchants, and traders in London, and others, subscribers to a British stock for a general insurance from fire in any part of England, praying to be incorporated for carrying on the said undertaking.

"13. Petition of several of his majesty's loyal subjects of the city of London and other parts of Great Britain, praying to be incorporated for carrying on a general insurance from losses by fire within the kingdom of England.

"14. Petition of Thomas Burges and others his majesty's subjects thereto subscribing, in behalf of themselves and others, subscribers to a fund of 1,200,000*l.* for carrying on a trade to his majesty's German dominions, praying to be incorporated by the name of the Harburg Company.

"15. Petition of Edward Jones, a dealer in timber, on behalf of himself and others, praying to be incorporated for the importation of timber from Germany.

"16. Petition of several merchants of London, praying a charter of incorporation for carrying on a salt-work.

"17. Petition of Captain Macphedris of London, merchant, on behalf of himself and several merchants, clothiers, hatters, dyers, and other traders, praying a charter of incorporation empowering them to raise a sufficient sum of money to purchase lands for planting and rearing a wood called madder, for the use of dyers.

"18. Petition of Joseph Galendo of London, snuff-maker, praying a patent for his invention to prepare and cure Virginia tobacco for snuff in Virginia, and making it into the same in all his majesty's dominions."

LIST OF BUBBLES

The following Bubble-Companies were by the same order declared to be illegal, and abolished accordingly:

1. For the importation of Swedish iron.

2. For supplying London with sea-coal. Capital, three millions.

3. For building and rebuilding houses throughout all England. Capital, three millions.

4. For making of muslin.

5. For carrying on and improving the British alum-works.

6. For effectually settling the island of Blanco and Sal Tartagus.

7. For supplying the town of Deal with fresh water.

8. For the importation of Flanders lace.

9. For improvement of lands in Great Britain. Capital, four millions.

10. For encouraging the breed of horses in England, and improving of glebe and church lands, and for repairing and rebuilding parsonage and vicarage houses.

11. For making of iron and steel in Great Britain.

12. For improving the land in the county of Flint. Capital, one million.

13. For purchasing lands to build on. Capital, two millions.

14. For trading in hair.

15. For erecting salt-works in Holy Island. Capital, two millions.

16. For buying and selling estates, and lending money on mortgage.

17. For carrying on an undertaking of great advantage; but nobody to know what it is.

18. For paving the streets of London. Capital, two millions.

19. For furnishing funerals to any part of Great Britain.

20. For buying and selling lands and lending money at interest. Capital, five millions.

21. For carrying on the royal fishery of Great Britain. Capital, ten millions.

22. For assuring of seamen's wages.

23. For erecting loan-offices for the assistance and encouragement of the industrious. Capital, two millions.

24. For purchasing and improving leaseable lands. Capital, four millions.

25. For importing pitch and tar, and other naval stores, from North Britain and America.

26. For the clothing, felt, and pantile trade.

27. For purchasing and improving a manor and royalty in Essex.

28. For insuring of horses. Capital, two millions.

29. For exporting the woollen manufacture, and importing copper, brass, and iron. Capital, four millions.

30. For a grand dispensary. Capital, three millions.

31. For erecting mills and purchasing lead-mines. Capital, two millions.

32. For improving the art of making soap.

33. For a settlement on the island of Santa Cruz.

34. For sinking pits and smelting lead ore in Derbyshire.

35. For making glass bottles and other glass.

36. For a wheel for perpetual motion. Capital, one million.

37. For improving of gardens.

38. For insuring and increasing children's fortunes.

39. For entering and loading goods at the Custom-house, and for negotiating business for merchants.

40. For carrying on a woollen manufacture in the north of England.

41. For importing walnut-trees from Virginia. Capital, two millions.

42. For making Manchester stuffs of thread and cotton.

43. For making Joppa and Castile soap.

44. For improving the wrought-iron and steel manufactures of this kingdom. Capital, four millions.

45. For dealing in lace, hollands, cambrics, lawns, &c. Capital, two millions.

46. For trading in and improving certain commodities of the produce of this kingdom, &c. Capital, three millions.

47. For supplying the London markets with cattle.

48. For making looking-glasses, coach-glasses, &c. Capital, two millions.

49. For working the tin and lead mines in Cornwall and Derbyshire.

50. For making rape-oil.

51. For importing beaver fur. Capital, two millions.

52. For making pasteboard and packing-paper.

53. For importing of oils and other materials used in the woollen manufacture.

54. For improving and increasing the silk manufactures.

55. For lending money on stock, annuities, tallies, &c.

56. For paying pensions to widows and others, at a small discount. Capital, two millions.

57. For improving malt liquors. Capital, four millions.

58. For a grand American fishery.

59. For purchasing and improving the fenny lands in Lincolnshire. Capital, two millions.

60. For improving the paper manufacture of Great Britain.

61. The Bottomry Company.

62. For drying malt by hot air.

63. For carrying on a trade in the river Oronooko.

64. For the more effectual making of baize, in Colchester and other parts of Great Britain.

65. For buying of naval stores, supplying the victualling, and paying the wages of the workmen.

66. For employing poor artificers, and furnishing merchants and others with watches.

67. For improvement of tillage and the breed of cattle.

68. Another for the improvement of our breed in horses.

69. Another for a horse-insurance.

70. For carrying on the corn trade of Great Britain.

71. For insuring to all masters and mistresses the losses they may sustain by servants. Capital, three millions.

72. For erecting houses or hospitals for taking in and maintaining illegitimate children. Capital, two millions.

TREE CARICATURE

73. For bleaching coarse sugars, without the use of fire or loss of substance.

74. For building turnpikes and wharfs in Great Britain.

75. For insuring from thefts and robberies.

76. For extracting silver from lead.

77. For making china and delft ware. Capital, one million.

78. For importing tobacco, and exporting it again to Sweden and the north of Europe. Capital, four millions.

79. For making iron with pit coal.

80. For furnishing the cities of London and Westminster with hay and straw. Capital, three millions.

81. For a sail and packing-cloth manufactory in Ireland.

82. For taking up ballast.

83. For buying and fitting out ships to suppress pirates.

84. For the importation of timber from Wales. Capital, two millions.

85. For rock-salt.

86. For the transmutation of quicksilver into a malleable fine metal.

Besides these bubbles, many others sprang up daily, in spite of the condemnation of the government and the ridicule of the still sane portion of the public. The print-shops teemed with caricatures, and the newspapers with epigrams and satires, upon the prevalent folly. An ingenious cardmaker published a pack of South-Sea playing-cards, which are now extremely rare, each card containing, besides the usual figures of a very small size, in one corner, a caricature of a bubble company, with appropriate verses underneath. One of the most famous bubbles was "Puckle's Machine Company," for discharging round and square cannon-balls and bullets, and making a total revolution in the art of war. Its pretensions to public favour were thus summed up on the eight of spades:

"A rare invention to destroy the crowd
Of fools at home instead of fools abroad.
Fear not, my friends, this terrible machine,
They're only wounded who have shares therein."

The nine of hearts was a caricature of the English Copper and Brass Company, with the following epigram:

> "The headlong fool that wants to be a swopper
> Of gold and silver coin for English copper,
> May, in Change Alley, prove himself an ass,
> And give rich metal for adultrate brass."

The eight of diamonds celebrated the company for the colonisation of Acadia, with this doggrel:

> "He that is rich and wants to fool away
> A good round sum in North America,
> Let him subscribe himself a headlong sharer,
> And asses' ears shall honour him or bearer."

And in a similar style every card of the pack exposed some knavish scheme, and ridiculed the persons who were its dupes. It was computed that the total amount of the sums proposed for carrying on these projects was upwards of three hundred millions sterling.

It is time, however, to return to the great South-Sea gulf, that swallowed the fortunes of so many thousands of the avaricious and the credulous. On the 29th of May, the stock had risen as high as five hundred, and about two-thirds of the government annuitants had exchanged the securities of the state for those of the South-Sea company. During the whole of the month of May the stock continued to rise, and on the 28th it was quoted at five hundred and fifty. In four days after this it took a prodigious leap, rising suddenly from five hundred and fifty to eight hundred and ninety. It was now the general opinion that the stock could rise no higher, and many persons took that opportunity of selling out, with a view of realising their profits. Many noblemen and persons in the train of the king, and about to accompany him to Hanover, were also anxious to sell out. So many sellers, and so few buyers, appeared in the Alley on the 3d of June, that the stock fell at once from eight hundred and ninety to six hundred and forty. The directors were alarmed, and gave their agents orders to buy. Their efforts succeeded. Towards evening, confidence was restored, and the stock advanced to seven hundred and fifty. It continued at this price, with some slight fluctuation, until the company closed their books on the 22d of June.

It would be needless and uninteresting to detail the various arts employed by the directors to keep up the price of stock. It will be sufficient to state that it finally rose to one thousand per cent. It was quoted at this price in the commencement of August. The bubble was then full-blown, and began to quiver and shake preparatory to its bursting.

Many of the government annuitants expressed dissatisfaction against the directors. They accused them of partiality in making out the lists for shares in each subscription. Further uneasiness was occasioned by its being generally known that Sir John Blunt the chairman, and some others, had sold out. During the whole of the month of August the stock fell, and on the 2d of September it was quoted at seven hundred only.

The state of things now became alarming. To prevent, if possible, the utter extinction of public confidence in their proceedings, the directors summoned a general court of the whole corporation, to meet in Merchant Tailors' Hall on the 8th of September. By nine o'clock in the morning, the room was filled to suffocation; Cheapside was blocked up by a crowd unable to gain admittance, and the greatest excitement prevailed. The directors and their friends mustered in great numbers. Sir John Fellowes, the sub-governor, was called to the chair. He acquainted the assembly with the cause of their meeting; read to them the several resolutions of the court of directors, and gave them an account of their proceedings; of the taking in the redeemable and unredeemable funds, and of the subscriptions in money. Mr. Secretary Craggs then made a short speech, wherein he commended the conduct of the directors, and urged that nothing could more effectually contribute to the bringing this scheme to perfection than union among themselves. He concluded with a motion for thanking the court of directors for their prudent and skilful management, and for desiring them to proceed in such manner as they should think most proper for the interest and advantage of the corporation. Mr. Hungerford, who had rendered himself very conspicuous in the House of Commons for his zeal in behalf of the South-Sea company, and who was shrewdly suspected to have been a considerable gainer by knowing the right time to sell out, was very magniloquent on this occasion. He said that he had seen the rise and fall, the decay and resurrection of many communities of this nature, but that, in his opinion, none had ever performed such wonderful things in so short a time as the South-Sea company. They had done more than the crown, the pulpit, or the bench could do. They had reconciled all parties in one common interest; they had laid asleep, if not wholly extinguished, all the domestic jars and animosities of the nation. By the rise of their stock, monied men had vastly increased their fortunes; country gentlemen had seen the value of their lands doubled and trebled in their hands. They had at the same time done good to the Church, not a few of the reverend clergy having got great sums by the project. In short, they had enriched the whole nation, and he hoped they had not forgotten themselves. There was some hissing at the latter part of this speech, which for the extravagance of its eulogy was not far removed from satire; but the directors and their friends, and all the winners in the room, applauded vehemently. The Duke of Portland spoke in a similar strain, and expressed his great wonder why any body should be dissatisfied; of course, he was a winner by his speculations, and in a condition similar to that of the fat alderman in *Joe Miller's Jests,* who, whenever he had eaten a good dinner, folded his hands upon his paunch, and expressed his doubts whether there could be a hungry man in the world.

Several resolutions were passed at this meeting, but they had no effect upon the public. Upon the very same evening the stock fell to six hundred and forty, and on the morrow to five hundred and forty. Day after day it continued to fall, until it was as low as four hundred. In a letter dated September 13th, from Mr. Broderick, M.P., to Lord Chancellor Middleton, and published in Coxe's *Walpole*, the former says: "Various are the conjectures why the South-Sea directors have suffered the cloud to break so early. I made no doubt but they would do so when they found it to their advantage. They have stretched credit so far beyond what it would bear, that specie proves insufficient to support it. Their most considerable men have drawn out, securing themselves by the losses of the deluded, thoughtless numbers, whose understandings have been overruled by avarice and the hope of making mountains out of mole-hills. Thousands of families will be reduced to beggary. The consternation is inexpressible—the rage beyond description, and the case altogether so desperate, that I do not see any plan or scheme so much as thought of for averting the blow; so that I cannot pretend to guess what is next to be done." Ten days afterwards, the stock still falling, he writes: "The company have yet come to no determination, for they are in such a wood that they know not which way to turn. By several gentlemen lately come to town, I perceive the very name of a South-Sea-man grows abominable in every country. A great many goldsmiths are already run off, and more will daily. I question whether one-third, nay, one-fourth of them can stand it. From the very beginning, I founded my judgment of the whole affair upon the unquestionable maxim, that ten millions (which is more than our running cash) could not circulate two hundred millions beyond which our paper credit extended. That, therefore, whenever that should become doubtful, be the cause what it would, our noble state machine must inevitably fall to the ground."

On the 12th of September, at the earnest solicitation of Mr. Secretary Craggs, several conferences were held between the directors of the South Sea and the directors of the Bank. A report which was circulated, that the latter had agreed to circulate six millions of the South-Sea company's bonds, caused the stock to rise to six hundred and seventy; but in the afternoon, as soon as the report was known to be groundless, the stock fell again to five hundred and eighty; the next day to five hundred and seventy, and so gradually to four hundred.*

The ministry were seriously alarmed at the aspect of affairs. The directors could not appear in the streets without being insulted; dangerous riots were every moment apprehended. Despatches were sent off to the king at Hanover, praying his immediate return. Mr. Walpole, who was staying at his country seat, was sent for, that he might employ his known influence with the directors of the Bank of England to induce them to accept the proposal made by the South-Sea company for circulating a number of their bonds.

The Bank was very unwilling to mix itself up with the affairs of the company; it dreaded being involved in calamities which it could not relieve, and received all overtures with visible reluctance. But the universal voice of the nation called upon it to come to the rescue. Every person of note in commercial politics was called in to advise in the emergency. A rough draft of a contract drawn up by Mr. Walpole was ultimately adopted as the basis of further negotiations, and the public alarm abated a little.

On the following day, the 20th of September, a general court of the South-Sea company was held at Merchant Tailors' Hall, in which resolutions were carried, empowering the directors to agree with the Bank of England, or any other persons, to circulate the company's bonds, or make any other agreement with the Bank which they should think proper. One of the speakers, a Mr. Pulteney, said it was most surprising to see the extraordinary panic which had seized upon the people. Men were running to and fro in alarm and terror,

---

* Gay (the poet), in that disastrous year, had a present from young Craggs of some South-Sea stock, and once supposed himself to be master of twenty thousand pounds. His friends persuaded him to sell his share, but he dreamed of dignity and splendour, and could not bear to obstruct his own fortune. He was then importuned to sell as much as would purchase a hundred a year for life, "which," says Fenton, "will make you sure of a clean shirt and a shoulder of mutton every day." This counsel was rejected; the profit and principal were lost, and Gay sunk under the calamity so low that his life became in danger.—*Johnson's Lives of the Poets.*

their imaginations filled with some great calamity, the form and dimensions of which nobody knew:

"Black it stood as night—
Fierce as ten furies—terrible as hell."

At a general court of the Bank of England, held two days afterwards, the governor informed them of the several meetings that had been held on the affairs of the South-Sea company, adding that the directors had not yet thought fit to come to any decision upon the matter. A resolution was then proposed, and carried without a dissentient voice, empowering the directors to agree with those of the South-Sea to circulate their bonds, to what sum, and upon what terms, and for what time, they might think proper.

Thus both parties were at liberty to act as they might judge best for the public interest. Books were opened at the Bank for a subscription of three millions for the support of public credit, on the usual terms of 15l. per cent deposit, 3l. per cent premium, and 5l. per cent interest. So great was the concourse of people in the early part of the morning, all eagerly bringing their money, that it was thought the subscription would be filled that day; but before noon the tide turned. In spite of all that could be done to prevent it, the South-Sea company's stock fell rapidly. Their bonds were in such discredit, that a run commenced upon the most eminent goldsmiths and bankers, some of whom, having lent out great sums upon South-Sea stock, were obliged to shut up their shops and abscond. The Sword-blade company, who had hitherto been the chief cashiers of the South-Sea company, stopped payment. This being looked upon as but the beginning of evil, occasioned a great run upon the bank, who were now obliged to pay out money much faster than they had received it upon the subscription in the morning. The day succeeding was a holiday (the 29th of September), and the Bank had a little breathing time. They bore up against the storm; but their former rivals, the South-Sea company, were wrecked upon it. Their stock fell to one hundred and fifty, and gradually, after various fluctuations, to one hundred and thirty-five.

The Bank finding they were not able to restore public confidence, and stem the tide of ruin, without running the risk of being swept away with those they intended to save, declined to carry out the agreement into which they had partially entered. They were under no obligation whatever to continue; for the so-called Bank contract was nothing more than the rough draft of an agreement, in which blanks had been left for several important particulars, and which contained no penalty for their secession. "And thus," to use the words of the Parliamentary History, "were seen, in the space of eight months, the rise, progress, and fall of that mighty fabric, which, being wound up by mysterious springs to a wonderful height, had fixed the eyes and expectations of all Europe, but whose foundation, being fraud, illusion, credulity, and infatuation, fell to the ground as soon as the artful management of its directors was discovered."

In the hey-day of its blood, during the progress of this dangerous delusion, the manners of the nation became sensibly corrupted. The parliamentary inquiry, set on foot to discover the delinquents, disclosed scenes of infamy, disgraceful alike to the morals of the offenders and the intellects of the people among whom they had arisen. It is a deeply interesting study to investigate all the evils that were the result. Nations, like individuals, cannot become desperate gamblers with impunity. Punishment is sure to overtake them sooner or later. A celebrated writer* is quite wrong when he says "that such an era as this is the most unfavourable for a historian; that no reader of sentiment and imagination can be entertained or interested by a detail of transactions such as these, which admit of no warmth, no colouring, no embellishment; a detail of which only serves to exhibit an inanimate picture of tasteless vice and mean degeneracy." On the contrary,—and Smollett might have discovered it, if he had been in the humour,—the subject is capable of inspiring as much interest as even a novelist can desire. Is there no warmth in the despair of a plundered people?—no life and animation in the picture which

* Smollett.

might be drawn of the woes of hundreds of impoverished and ruined families? of the wealthy of yesterday become the beggars of to-day? of the powerful and influential changed into exiles and outcasts, and the voice of self-reproach and imprecation resounding from every corner of the land? Is it a dull or uninstructive picture to see a whole people shaking suddenly off the trammels of reason, and running wild after a golden vision, refusing obstinately to believe that it is not real, till, like a deluded hind running after an *ignis fatuus*, they are plunged into a quagmire? But in this false spirit has history too often been written. The intrigues of unworthy courtiers to gain the favour of still more unworthy kings, or the records of murderous battles and sieges, have been dilated on, and told over and over again, with all the eloquence of style and all the charms of fancy; while the circumstances which have most deeply affected the morals and welfare of the people have been passed over with but slight notice, as dry and dull, and capable of neither warmth nor colouring.

During the progress of this famous bubble, England presented a singular spectacle. The public mind was in a state of unwholesome fermentation. Men were no longer satisfied with the slow but sure profits of cautious industry. The hope of boundless wealth for the morrow made them heedless and extravagant for to-day. A luxury, till then unheard of, was introduced, bringing in its train a corresponding laxity of morals. The overbearing insolence of ignorant men, who had arisen to sudden wealth by successful gambling, made men of true gentility of mind and manners blush that gold should have power to raise the unworthy in the scale of society. The haughtiness of some of these "cyphering cits," as they were termed by Sir Richard Steele, was remembered against them in the day of their adversity. In the parliamentary inquiry, many of the directors suffered more for their insolence than for their peculation. One of them, who, in the full-blown pride of an ignorant rich man, had said that he would feed his horse upon gold, was reduced almost to bread and water for himself; every haughty look, every overbearing speech, was set down, and repaid them a hundredfold in poverty and humiliation.

The state of matters all over the country was so alarming, that George I. shortened his intended stay in Hanover, and returned in all haste to England. He arrived on the 11th of November, and parliament was summoned to meet on the 8th of December. In the mean time, public meetings were held in every considerable town of the empire, at which petitions were adopted, praying the vengeance of the legislature upon the South-Sea directors, who, by their fraudulent practices, had brought the nation to the brink of ruin. Nobody seemed to imagine that the nation itself was as culpable as the South-Sea company. Nobody blamed the credulity and avarice of the people—the degrading lust of gain, which had swallowed up every nobler quality in the national character, or the infatuation which had made the multitude run their heads with such frantic eagerness into the net held out for them by scheming projectors. These things were never mentioned. The people were a simple, honest, hard-working people, ruined by a gang of robbers, who were to be hanged, drawn, and quartered without mercy.

This was the almost unanimous feeling of the country. The two Houses of Parliament were not more reasonable. Before the guilt of the South-Sea directors was known, punishment was the only cry. The king, in his speech from the throne, expressed his hope that they would remember that all their prudence, temper, and resolution were necessary to find out and apply the proper remedy for their misfortunes. In the debate on the answer to the address, several speakers indulged in the most violent invectives against the directors of the South-Sea project. The Lord Molesworth was particularly vehement.

"It had been said by some, that there was no law to punish the directors of the South-Sea company, who were justly looked upon as the authors of the present misfortunes of the state. In his opinion, they ought upon this occasion to follow the example of the ancient Romans, who, having no law against parricide, because their legislators supposed no son could be so unnaturally wicked as to embrue his hands in his father's blood, made a law to punish this heinous crime as soon as it was committed. They adjudged the guilty wretch to be sewn in a sack, and thrown alive into the Tiber. He looked upon the contrivers and executors of the villanous South-Sea scheme as the parricides of their country, and should be satisfied to see them tied in like manner in sacks, and thrown into the Thames." Other members spoke with as much want of temper and discretion. Mr. Walpole was more moderate. He recommended that their first care should be to restore public credit. "If the city of London were on fire, all wise men would aid in extinguishing the flames, and preventing the spread of the conflagration, before they inquired after the incendiaries. Public credit had received a dangerous wound, and lay bleeding, and they ought to apply a speedy remedy to it. It was time enough to punish the assassin afterwards." On the 9th of December, an address, in answer to his majesty's speech, was agreed upon, after an amendment, which was carried without a division, that words should be added expressive of the determination of the House not only to seek a remedy for the national distresses, but to punish the authors of them.

The inquiry proceeded rapidly. The directors were ordered to lay before the House a full account of all their proceedings. Resolutions were passed to the effect that the calamity was mainly owing to the vile arts of stock-jobbers, and that nothing could tend more to the re-establishment of public credit than a law to prevent this infamous practice. Mr. Walpole then rose, and said, that "as he had previously hinted, he had spent some time upon a scheme for restoring public credit, but that the execution of it depending upon a position which had been laid down as fundamental, he thought it proper, before he opened out his scheme, to be informed whether he might rely upon that foundation. It was, whether the subscription of public debts and encumbrances, money subscriptions, and other contracts, made with the South-Sea company, should remain in the present state?" This question occasioned an animated debate. It was finally agreed, by a majority of

259 against 117, that all these contracts should remain in their present state, unless altered for the relief of the proprietors by a general court of the South-Sea company, or set aside by due course of law. On the following day, Mr. Walpole laid before a committee of the whole house his scheme for the restoration of public credit, which was, in substance, to engraft nine millions of South-Sea Stock into the Bank of England, and the same sum into the East India company upon certain conditions. The plan was favourably received by the House. After some few objections, it was ordered that proposals should be received from the two great corporations. They were both unwilling to lend their aid, and the plan met with a warm but fruitless opposition at the general courts summoned for the purpose of deliberating upon it. They, however, ultimately agreed upon the terms on which they would consent to circulate the South-Sea bonds, and their report being presented to the committee, a bill was brought in under the superintendence of Mr. Walpole, and safely carried through both Houses of Parliament.

A bill was at the same time brought in for restraining the South-Sea directors, governor, sub-governor, treasurer, cashier, and clerks from leaving the kingdom for a twelvemonth, and for discovering their estates and effects, and preventing them from transporting or alienating the same. All the most influential members of the House supported the bill. Mr. Shippen, seeing Mr. Secretary Craggs in his place, and believing the injurious rumours that were afloat of that minister's conduct in the South-Sea business, determined to touch him to the quick. He said he was glad to see a British House of Commons resuming its pristine vigour and spirit, and acting with so much unanimity for the public good. It was necessary to secure the persons and estates of the South-Sea directors and their officers; "but," he added, looking fixedly at Mr. Craggs as he spoke, "there were other men in high station, whom, in time, he would not be afraid to name, who were no less guilty than the directors." Mr. Craggs arose in great wrath, and said, that if the inuendo were directed against him, he was ready to give satisfaction to any man who questioned him, either in the House or out of it. Loud cries of order immediately arose on every side. In the midst of the uproar, Lord Molesworth got up, and expressed his wonder at the boldness of Mr. Craggs in challenging the whole House of Commons. He, Lord Molesworth, though somewhat old, past sixty, would answer Mr. Craggs whatever he had to say in the House, and he trusted there were plenty of young men beside him, who would not be afraid to look Mr. Craggs in the face out of the House. The cries of order again resounded from every side; the members arose simultaneously; everybody seemed to be vociferating at once. The Speaker in vain called order. The confusion lasted several minutes, during which Lord Molesworth and Mr. Craggs were almost the only members who kept their seats. At last, the call for Mr. Craggs became so violent, that he thought proper to submit to the universal feeling of the House, and explain his unparliamentary expression. He said, that by giving satisfaction to the impugners of his conduct in that House, he did not mean that he would fight, but that he would explain his conduct. Here the matter ended, and the House proceeded to debate in what manner they should conduct their inquiry into the affairs of the South-Sea company, whether in a grand or a select committee. Ultimately, a secret committee of thirteen was appointed, with power to send for persons, papers, and records.

The Lords were as zealous and as hasty as the Commons. The Bishop of Rochester said the scheme had been like a pestilence. The Duke of Wharton said the House ought to shew no respect of persons; that, for his part, he would give up the dearest friend he had, if he had been engaged in the project. The nation had been plundered in a most shameful and flagrant manner, and he would go as far as anybody in the punishment of the offenders. Lord Stanhope said, that every farthing possessed by the criminals, whether directors or not directors, ought to be confiscated, to make good the public losses.

During all this time the public excitement was extreme. We learn from Coxe's *Walpole,* that the very name of a South-

Sea director was thought to be synonymous with every species of fraud and villany. Petitions from counties, cities, and boroughs, in all parts of the kingdom, were presented, crying for the justice due to an injured nation and the punishment of the villanous peculators. Those moderate men, who would not go to extreme lengths, even in the punishment of the guilty, were accused of being accomplices, were exposed to repeated insults and virulent invectives, and devoted, both in anonymous letters and public writings, to the speedy vengeance of an injured people. The accusations against Mr. Aislabie, Chancellor of the Exchequer, and Mr. Craggs, another member of the ministry, were so loud, that the House of Lords resolved to proceed at once into the investigation concerning them. It was ordered, on the 21st of January, that all brokers concerned in the South-Sea scheme should lay before the House an account of the stock or subscriptions bought or sold by them for any of the officers of the Treasury or Exchequer, or in trust for any of them, since Michaelmas 1719. When this account was delivered, it appeared that large quantities of stock had been transferred to the use of Mr. Aislabie. Five of the South-Sea directors, including Mr. Edward Gibbon, the grandfather of the celebrated historian, were ordered into the custody of the black rod. Upon a motion made by Earl Stanhope, it was unanimously resolved, that the taking in or giving credit for stock without a valuable consideration actually paid or sufficiently secured; or the purchasing stock by any director or agent of the South-Sea company, for the use or benefit of any member of the administration, or any member of either House of Parliament, during such time as the South-Sea bill was yet pending in Parliament, was a notorious and dangerous corruption. Another resolution was passed a few days afterwards, to the effect that several of the directors and officers of the company having, in a clandestine manner, sold their own stock to the company, had been guilty of a notorious fraud and breach of trust, and had thereby mainly caused the unhappy turn of affairs that had so much affected public credit. Mr. Aislabie resigned his office as Chancellor of the Exchequer, and absented himself from parliament, until the formal inquiry into his individual guilt was brought under the consideration of the legislature.

In the mean time, Knight, the treasurer of the company, and who was entrusted with all the dangerous secrets of the dishonest directors, packed up his books and documents and made his escape from the country. He embarked in disguise, in a small boat on the river, and proceeding to a vessel hired for the purpose, was safely conveyed to Calais. The Committee of Secrecy informed the House of the circumstance, when it was resolved unanimously that two addresses should be presented to the king; the first praying that he would issue a proclamation offering a reward for the apprehension of Knight; and the second, that he would give immediate orders to stop the ports, and to take effectual care of the coasts, to prevent the said Knight, or any other officers of the South-Sea company, from escaping out of the kingdom. The ink was hardly dry upon these addresses before they were carried to the king by Mr. Methuen, deputed by the House for that purpose. The same evening a royal proclamation was issued, offering a reward of two thousand pounds for the apprehension of Knight. The Commons ordered the doors of the House to be locked, and the keys to be placed on the table. General Ross, one of the members of the Committee of Secrecy, acquainted them that they had already discovered a train of the deepest villany and fraud that hell had ever contrived to ruin a nation, which in due time they would lay before the House. In the mean time, in order to a further discovery, the Committee thought it highly necessary to secure the persons of some of the directors and principal South-Sea officers, and to seize their papers. A motion to this effect having been made, was carried unanimously. Sir Robert Chaplin, Sir Theodore Janssen, Mr. Sawbridge, and Mr. F. Eyles, members of the House, and directors of the South-Sea company, were summoned to appear in their places, and answer for their corrupt practices. Sir Theodore Janssen and Mr. Sawbridge answered to their names, and endeavoured to exculpate themselves. The House heard them patiently, and then ordered them to withdraw. A motion was then made, and carried *nemine contradicente*, that they had been guilty of a notorious breach of trust—had occasioned much loss to great numbers of his majesty's subjects, and had highly prejudiced the public credit. It was then ordered that, for their offence, they should be expelled the House, and taken into custody of the sergeant-at-arms. Sir Robert Chaplin and Mr. Eyles, attending in their places four days afterwards, were also expelled the House. It was resolved at the same time to address the king to give directions to his ministers at foreign courts to make application for Knight, that he might be delivered up to the English authorities, in case he took refuge in any of their dominions. The king at once agreed, and messengers were despatched to all parts of the continent the same night.

Among the directors taken into custody was Sir John Blunt, the man whom popular opinion has generally accused of having been the original author and father of the scheme. This man, we are informed by Pope, in his epistle to Allen Lord Bathurst, was a Dissenter, of a most religious deportment, and professed to be a great believer.* He constantly declaimed against the luxury and corruption of the age, the partiality of parliaments, and the misery of party-spirit. He

---

* " 'God cannot love,' says Blunt, with tearless eyes,
'The wretch he starves,' and piously denies. . . . .
Much-injur'd Blunt! why bears he Britain's hate?
A wizard told him in these words our fate:
'At length corruption, like a general flood,
So long by watchful ministers withstood,
Shall deluge all; and avarice, creeping on,
Spread like a low-born mist, and blot the sun;
Statesman and patriot ply alike the stocks,
Peeress and butler share alike the box,
And judges job, and bishops bite the town,
And mighty dukes pack cards for half-a-crown:
See Britain sunk in Lucre's sordid charms
And France revenged on Anne's and Edward's arms!'
'Twas no court-badge, great Scrivener! fir'd thy brain,
Nor lordly luxury, nor city gain:
No, 'twas thy righteous end, asham'd to see
Senates degen'rate, patriots disagree,
And nobly wishing party-rage to cease,
To buy both sides, and give thy country peace."
Pope's Epistle to Allen Lord Bathurst.

was particularly eloquent against avarice in great and noble persons. He was originally a scrivener, and afterwards became not only a director, but the most active manager of the South-Sea company. Whether it was during his career in this capacity that he first began to declaim against the avarice of the great, we are not informed. He certainly must have seen enough of it to justify his severest anathema; but if the preacher had himself been free from the vice he condemned, his declamations would have had a better effect. He was brought up in custody to the bar of the House of Lords, and underwent a long examination. He refused to answer several important questions. He said he had been examined already by a committee of the House of Commons, and as he did not remember his answers, and might contradict himself, he refused to answer before another tribunal. This declaration, in itself an indirect proof of guilt, occasioned some commotion in the House. He was again asked peremptorily whether he had ever sold any portion of the stock to any member of the administration, or any member of either House of Parliament, to facilitate the passing of the bill. He again declined to answer. He was anxious, he said, to treat the House with all possible respect, but he thought it hard to be compelled to accuse himself. After several ineffectual attempts to refresh his memory, he was directed to withdraw. A violent discussion ensued between the friends and opponents of the ministry. It was asserted that the administration were no strangers to the convenient taciturnity of Sir John Blunt. The Duke of Wharton made a reflection upon the Earl Stanhope, which the latter warmly resented. He spoke under great excitement, and with such vehemence as to cause a sudden determination of blood to the head. He felt himself so ill that he was obliged to leave the House and retire to his chamber. He was cupped immediately, and also let blood on the following morning, but with slight relief. The fatal result was not anticipated. Towards evening he became drowsy, and turning himself on his face, expired. The sudden death of this statesman caused great grief to the nation. George I. was exceedingly affected, and shut himself up for some hours in his closet, inconsolable for his loss.

Knight, the treasurer of the company, was apprehended at Tirlemont, near Liege, by one of the secretaries of Mr. Leathes, the British resident at Brussels, and lodged in the citadel of Antwerp. Repeated applications were made to the court of Austria to deliver him up, but in vain. Knight threw himself upon the protection of the states of Brabant, and demanded to be tried in that country. It was a privilege granted to the states of Brabant by one of the articles of the *Joyeuse Entrée*, that every criminal apprehended in that country should be tried in that country. The states insisted on their privilege, and refused to deliver Knight to the British authorities. The latter did not cease their solicitations; but in the mean time, Knight escaped from the citadel.

On the 16th of February the Committee of Secrecy made their first report to the House. They stated that their inquiry had been attended with numerous difficulties and embarrassments; every one they had examined had endeavoured, as far as in him lay, to defeat the ends of justice. In some of the books produced before them, false and fictitious entries had been made; in others, there were entries of money with blanks for the name of the stockholders. There were frequent erasures and alterations, and in some of the books leaves were torn out. They also found that some books of great importance had been destroyed altogether, and that some had been taken away or secreted. At the very entrance into their inquiry, they had observed that the matters referred to them were of great variety and extent. Many persons had been entrusted with various parts in the execution of the law, and under colour thereof had acted in an unwarrantable manner, in disposing of the properties of many thousands of persons amounting to many millions of money. They discovered that, before the South-Sea Act was passed, there was an entry in the company's books of the sum of 1,259,325*l*., upon account of stock stated to have been sold to the amount of 574,500*l.* This stock was all fictitious, and had been disposed of with a view to promote the passing of the bill. It was noted as sold on various days, and at various prices, from 150 to 325 per cent. Being surprised to see so large an account disposed of at a time when the company were not empowered to increase their capital, the Committee determined to investigate most carefully the whole transaction. The governor, sub-governor, and several directors were brought before them, and examined rigidly. They found that, at the time these entries were made, the company was not in possession of such a quantity of stock, having in their own right only a small quantity, not exceeding thirty thousand pounds at the utmost. Pursuing the inquiry, they found that this amount of stock was to be esteemed as taken in or holden by the company for the benefit of the pretended purchasers, although no mutual agreement was made for its delivery or acceptance at any certain time. No money was paid down, nor any deposit or security whatever given to the company by the supposed purchasers; so that if the stock had fallen, as might have been expected had the act not passed, they would have sustained no loss. If, on the contrary, the price of stock advanced (as it actually did by the success of the scheme), the difference by the advanced price was to be made good to them. Accordingly, after the passing of the act, the account of stock was made up and adjusted with Mr. Knight, and the pretended purchasers were paid the difference out of the company's cash. This fictitious stock, which had been chiefly at the disposal of Sir John Blunt, Mr. Gibbon, and Mr. Knight, was distributed among several members of the government and their connexions, by way of bribe, to facilitate the passing of the bill. To the Earl of Sunderland was assigned 50,000*l.* of this stock; to the Duchess of Kendal, 10,000*l.*; to the Countess of Platen, 10,000*l.*; to her two nieces, 10,000*l.*; to Mr. Secretary Craggs, 30,000*l.*; to Mr. Charles Stanhope (one of the secretaries of the Treasury), 10,000*l.*; to the Sword-blade company, 50,000*l.* It also appeared that Mr. Stanhope had received the enormous sum of 250,000*l.* as the difference in the price of some stock, through the hands of Turner, Caswall, and Co., but that his name had been partly erased from their books, and altered to Stangape. Aislabie, the Chancellor of the Exchequer, had made profits still more abominable. He had an account with the same firm, who were also South-Sea directors, to the amount of 794,451*l*. He had, besides, advised the company to make their second subscription one million and a half, instead of a million, by their own authority, and without any warrant. The third subscription had been conducted in a manner as disgraceful. Mr. Aislabie's name was down for 70,000*l*.; Mr. Craggs, senior, for 659,000*l*.; the Earl of Sunderland's for 160,000*l*.; and Mr. Stanhope for 47,000*l*. This report was succeeded by six others, less important. At the end of the last, the committee declared, that the absence of Knight, who had been principally entrusted, prevented them from carrying on their inquiries.

The first report was ordered to be printed, and taken into consideration on the next day but one succeeding. After a very angry and animated debate, a series of resolutions were agreed to, condemnatory of the conduct of the directors, of the members of the parliament and of the administration concerned with them; and declaring that they ought, each and all, to make satisfaction out of their own estates for the injury they had done the public. Their practices were declared to be corrupt, infamous, and dangerous; and a bill was ordered to be brought in for the relief of the unhappy sufferers.

Mr. Charles Stanhope was the first person brought to account for his share in these transactions. He urged in his defence that, for some years past, he had lodged all the money he was possessed of in Mr. Knight's hands, and whatever stock Mr. Knight had taken in for him, he had paid a valuable consideration for it. As for the stock that had been bought for him by Turner, Caswall, and Co., he knew nothing about it. Whatever had been done in that matter was done without his authority, and he could not be responsible for it. Turner and Co. took the latter charge upon themselves; but it was notorious to every unbiassed and unprejudiced person that Mr. Stanhope was a gainer of the 250,000*l*. which lay in the hands of that firm to his credit. He was, however, acquitted by a majority of three only. The greatest exertions were made to screen him. Lord Stanhope, the son of the

Earl of Chesterfield, went round to the wavering members, using all the eloquence he was possessed of to induce them either to vote for the acquittal, or to absent themselves from the House. Many weak-headed country gentlemen were led astray by his persuasions, and the result was as already stated. The acquittal caused the greatest discontent throughout the country. Mobs of a menacing character assembled in different parts of London; fears of riots were generally entertained, especially as the examination of a still greater delinquent was expected by many to have a similar termination. Mr. Aislabie, whose high office and deep responsibilities should have kept him honest, even had native principle been insufficient, was very justly regarded as perhaps the greatest criminal of all. His case was entered into on the day succeeding the acquittal of Mr. Stanhope. Great excitement prevailed, and the lobbies and avenues of the House were beset by crowds impatient to know the result. The debate lasted the whole day. Mr. Aislabie found few friends: his guilt was so apparent and so heinous that nobody had courage to stand up in his favour. It was finally resolved, without a dissentient voice, that Mr. Aislabie had encouraged and promoted the destructive execution of the South-Sea scheme with a view to his own exorbitant profit, and had combined with the directors in their pernicious practices, to the ruin of the public trade and credit of the kingdom: that he should for his offences be ignominiously expelled from the House of Commons, and committed a close prisoner to the Tower of London; that he should be restrained from going out of the kingdom for a whole year, or till the end of the next session of parliament; and that he should make out a correct account of all his estate, in order that it might be applied to the relief of those who had suffered by his mal-practices.

This verdict caused the greatest joy. Though it was delivered at half-past twelve at night, it soon spread over the city. Several persons illuminated their houses in token of their joy. On the following day, when Mr. Aislabie was conveyed to the Tower, the mob assembled on Tower-hill with the intention of hooting and pelting him. Not succeeding in this, they kindled a large bonfire, and danced around it in the exuberance of their delight. Several bonfires were made in other places; London presented the appearance of a holiday, and people congratulated one another as if they had just escaped from some great calamity. The rage upon the acquittal of Mr. Stanhope had grown to such a height, that none could tell where it would have ended, had Mr. Aislabie met with the like indulgence.

To increase the public satisfaction, Sir George Caswall, of the firm of Turner, Caswall, and Co., was expelled from the House on the following day, committed to the Tower, and ordered to refund the sum of 250,000*l.*

That part of the report of the Committee of Secrecy which related to the Earl of Sunderland was next taken into consideration. Every effort was made to clear his lordship from the imputation. As the case against him rested chiefly on the evidence extorted from Sir John Blunt, great pains were taken to make it appear that Sir John's word was not to be believed, especially in a matter affecting the honour of a peer and privy councillor. All the friends of the ministry rallied around the earl, it being generally reported that a verdict of guilty against him would bring a Tory ministry into power. He was eventually acquitted by a majority of 233 against 172; but the country was convinced of his guilt. The greatest indignation was everywhere expressed, and menacing mobs again assembled in London. Happily no disturbance took place.

This was the day on which Mr. Craggs the elder expired. The morrow had been appointed for the consideration of his case. It was very generally believed that he had poisoned himself. It appeared, however, that grief for the loss of his son, one of the secretaries of the Treasury, who had died five weeks previously of the small-pox, preyed much on his mind. For this son, dearly beloved, he had been amassing vast heaps of riches: he had been getting money, but not honestly; and he for whose sake he had bartered his honour and sullied his fame was now no more. The dread of further exposure increased his trouble of mind, and ultimately brought on an apoplectic fit, in which he expired. He left a fortune of a million and a half, which was afterwards confiscated for the benefit of the sufferers by the unhappy delusion he had been so mainly instrumental in raising.

One by one the case of every director of the company was taken into consideration. A sum amounting to two millions and fourteen thousand pounds was confiscated from their estates towards repairing the mischief they had done, each man being allowed a certain residue in proportion to his conduct and circumstances, with which he might begin the world anew. Sir John Blunt was only allowed 5000*l.* out of his fortune of upwards of 183,000*l.*; Sir John Fellows was allowed 10,000*l.* out of 243,000*l.*; Sir Theodore Janssen, 50,000*l.* out of 243,000*l.*; Mr. Edward Gibbon, 10,000*l.* out of 106,000*l.*; Sir John Lambert, 5000*l.* out of 72,000*l.* Others, less deeply involved, were treated with greater liberality. Gibbon, the historian, whose grandfather was the Mr. Edward Gibbon so severely mulcted, has given, in the *Memoirs of his Life and Writings,* an interesting account of the proceedings in parliament at this time. He owns that he is not an unprejudiced witness; but, as all the writers from which it is possible to extract any notice of the proceedings of these disastrous years were prejudiced on the other side, the statements of the great historian become of additional value. If only on the principle of *audi alteram partem,* his opinion is entitled to consideration. "In the year 1716," he says, "my grandfather was elected one of the directors of the South-Sea company, and his books exhibited the proof that before his acceptance of that fatal office, he had acquired an independent fortune of 60,000*l.* But his fortune was overwhelmed in the shipwreck of the year 1720, and the labours of thirty years were blasted in a single day. Of the use or abuse of the South-Sea scheme, of the guilt or innocence of my grandfather and his brother directors, I am neither a competent nor a disinterested judge. Yet the equity of modern times must condemn the violent and arbitrary proceedings, which would have disgraced the cause of justice, and rendered injustice still more odious. No sooner had the nation awakened from its golden dream, than a popular and even a parliamentary clamour demanded its victims; but it was acknowledged on all sides, that the directors, however guilty, could not be touched by any known laws of the land. The intemperate notions of Lord Molesworth were not literally acted on; but a bill of pains and penalties was introduced—a retroactive statute, to punish the offences which did not exist at the time they were committed. The legislature restrained the persons of the directors, imposed an exorbitant security for their appearance, and marked their character with a previous note of ignominy. They were compelled to deliver, upon oath, the strict value of their estates, and were disabled from making any transfer or alienation of any part of their property. Against a bill of pains and penalties, it is the common right of every subject to be heard by his counsel at the bar. They prayed to be heard. Their prayer was refused, and their oppressors, who required no evidence, would listen to no defence. It had been at first proposed, that one-eighth of their respective estates should be allowed for the future support of the directors; but it was especially urged that, in the various shades of opulence and guilt, such a proportion would be too light for many, and for some might possibly be too heavy. The character and conduct of each man were separately weighed; but, instead of the calm solemnity of a judicial inquiry, the fortune and honour of thirty-three Englishmen were made the topics of hasty conversation, the sport of a lawless majority; and the basest member of the committee, by a malicious word or a silent vote, might indulge his general spleen or personal animosity. Injury was aggravated by insult, and insult was embittered by pleasantry. Allowances of 20*l.* or 1*s.* were facetiously moved. A vague report that a director had formerly been concerned in another project, by which some unknown persons had lost their money, was admitted as a proof of his actual guilt. One man was ruined because he had dropped a foolish speech, that his horses should feed upon gold; another, because he was grown so proud, that one day, at the Treasury, he had refused a civil answer to persons much above him. All were condemned, absent and unheard, in arbitrary fines and forfeitures, which swept away the greatest part of their substance. Such bold oppression can scarcely be shielded by the omnipotence of parliament. My grandfather could not expect to be treated with more lenity than his companions. His Tory principles and connexions rendered him obnoxious to the ruling powers. His name was reported in a suspicious secret. His well-known abilities could not plead the excuse of ignorance or error. In the first proceedings against the South-Sea directors, Mr. Gibbon was one of the first taken into custody, and in the final sentence the measure of his fine proclaimed him eminently guilty. The total estimate, which he delivered on oath to the House of Commons, amounted to 106,543*l.* 5*s.* 6*d.,* exclusive of antecedent settlements. Two different allowances of 15,000*l.* and of 10,000*l.* were moved for Mr. Gibbon; but on the question being put, it was carried without a division for the smaller sum. On these ruins, with the skill and credit of which parliament had not been able to despoil him, my grandfather, at a mature age, erected the edifice of a new fortune. The labours of sixteen years were amply rewarded; and I have reason to believe that the second structure was not much inferior to the first."

The next consideration of the legislature, after the punishment of the directors, was to restore public credit. The scheme of Walpole had been found insufficient, and had fallen into disrepute. A computation was made of the whole capital stock of the South-Sea company at the end of the year 1720. It was found to amount to thirty-seven millions eight hundred thousand pounds, of which the stock allotted to all the proprietors only amounted to twenty-four millions five hundred thousand pounds. The remainder of thirteen millions three hundred thousand pounds belonged to the company in their corporate capacity, and was the profit they had made by the national delusion. Upwards of eight millions of this were taken from the company, and divided among the proprietors and subscribers generally, making a dividend of about 33*l.* 6*s.* 8*d.* per cent. This was a great relief. It was further ordered, that such persons as had borrowed money from the South-Sea company upon stock actually transferred and pledged at the time of borrowing to or for the use of the company, should be free from all demands, upon payment of ten per cent of the sums so borrowed. They had lent about eleven millions in this manner, at a time when prices were unnaturally raised; and they now received back one million one hundred thousand, when prices had sunk to their ordinary level.

But it was a long time before public credit was thoroughly restored. Enterprise, like Icarus, had soared too high, and melted the wax of her wings; like Icarus, she had fallen into a sea, and learned, while floundering in its waves, that her proper element was the solid ground. She has never since attempted so high a flight.

In times of great commercial prosperity there has been a tendency to over-speculation on several occasions since then. The success of one project generally produces others of a similar kind. Popular imitativeness will always, in a trading nation, seize hold of such successes, and drag a community too anxious for profits into an abyss from which extrication is difficult. Bubble companies, of a kind similar to those engendered by the South-Sea project, lived their little day in the famous year of the panic, 1825. On that occasion, as in 1720, knavery gathered a rich harvest from cupidity, but both suffered when the day of reckoning came. The schemes of the year 1836 threatened, at one time, results as disastrous; but they were happily averted before it was too late.*

* The South-Sea project remained until 1845 the greatest example in British history of the infatuation of the people for commercial gambling. The first edition of these volumes was published some time before the outbreak of the Great Railway Mania of that and the following year.

THE TULIPOMANIA

Quis furor, ô cives!—*Lucan.*

THE tulip—so named, it is said, from a Turkish word, signifying a turban—was introduced into western Europe about the middle of the sixteenth century. Conrad Gesner, who claims the merit of having brought it into repute,—little dreaming of the commotion it was shortly afterwards to make in the world,—says that he first saw it in the year 1559, in a garden at Augsburg, belonging to the learned Counsellor Herwart, a man very famous in his day for his collection of rare exotics. The bulbs were sent to this gentleman by a friend at Constantinople, where the flower had long been a favourite. In the course of ten or eleven years after this period, tulips were much sought after by the wealthy, especially in Holland and Germany. Rich people at Amsterdam sent for the bulbs direct to Constantinople, and paid the most extravagant prices for them. The first roots planted in England were brought from Vienna in 1600. Until the year 1634 the tulip annually increased in reputation, until it was deemed a proof of bad taste in any man of fortune to be without a collection of them. Many learned men, including Pompeius de Angelis, and the celebrated Lipsius of Leyden, the author of the treatise "De Constantia," were passionately fond of tulips. The rage for possessing them soon caught the middle classes of society, and merchants and shopkeepers, even of moderate means, began to vie with each other in the rarity of these flowers and the preposterous prices they paid for them. A trader at Harlaem was known to pay one-half of his fortune for a single root, not with the design of selling it again at a profit, but to keep in his own conservatory for the admiration of his acquaintance.

One would suppose that there must have been some great virtue in this flower to have made it so valuable in the eyes of so prudent a people as the Dutch; but it has neither the beauty nor the perfume of the rose—hardly the beauty of the "sweet, sweet-pea;" neither is it as enduring as either. Cowley, it is true, is loud in its praise. He says—

> "The tulip next appeared, all over gay,
>   But wanton, full of pride, and full of play;
>   The world can't show a dye but here has place;
>   Nay, by new mixtures, she can change her face;
>   Purple and gold are both beneath her care,
>   The richest needlework she loves to wear;
>   Her only study is to please the eye,
>   And to outshine the rest in finery."

This, though not very poetical, is the description of a poet. Beckmann, in his *History of Inventions*, paints it with more fidelity, and in prose more pleasing than Cowley's poetry. He says, "There are few plants which acquire, through accident, weakness, or disease, so many variegations as the tulip. When uncultivated, and in its natural state, it is almost of one colour, has large leaves, and an extraordinarily long stem. When it has been weakened by cultivation, it becomes more agreeable in the eyes of the florist. The petals are then paler, smaller, and more diversified in hue; and the leaves acquire a softer green colour. Thus this masterpiece of culture, the more beautiful it turns, grows so much the weaker, so that, with the greatest skill and most careful attention, it can scarcely be transplanted, or even kept alive."

Many persons grow insensibly attached to that which gives them a great deal of trouble, as a mother often loves her sick and ever-ailing child better than her more healthy offspring. Upon the same principle we must account for the unmerited encomia lavished upon these fragile blossoms. In 1634, the rage among the Dutch to possess them was so great that the ordinary industry of the country was neglected, and the population, even to its lowest dregs, embarked in the tulip trade. As the mania increased, prices augmented, until, in the year 1635, many persons were known to invest a fortune of 100,000 florins in the purchase of forty roots. It then became necessary to sell them by their weight in *perits,* a small weight less than a grain. A tulip of the species called *Admiral Liefken,* weighing 400 *perits,* was worth 4400 florins; an *Admiral Van der Eyck,* weighing 446 *perits,* was worth 1260 florins; a *Childer* of 106 *perits* was worth 1615 florins; a *Viceroy* of 400 *perits,* 3000 florins; and, most precious of all, a *Semper Augustus,* weighing 200 *perits,* was thought to be very cheap at 5500 florins. The latter was much sought after, and even an inferior bulb might command a price of 2000 florins. It is related that, at one time, early in 1636, there were only two roots of this description to be had in all Holland, and those not of the best. One was in the possession of a dealer in Amsterdam, and the other in Harlaem. So anxious were the speculators to obtain them, that one person offered the fee-simple of twelve acres of building-ground for the Harlaem tulip. That of Amsterdam was bought for 4600 florins, a new carriage, two grey horses, and a complete set of harness. Munting, an industrious author of that day, who wrote a folio volume of one thousand pages upon the tulipomania, has preserved the following list of the various articles, and their value, which were delivered for one single root of the rare species called the *Viceroy:*

	florins
Two lasts of wheat	448
Four lasts of rye	558
Four fat oxen	480
Eight fat swine	240
Twelve fat sheep	120
Two Hogsheads of wine	70
Four tuns of beer	32
Two tuns of butter	192
One thousand lbs. of cheese	120
A complete bed	100
A suit of clothes	80
A silver drinking-cup	60
	2500

People who had been absent from Holland, and whose chance it was to return when this folly was at its maximum, were sometimes led into awkward dilemmas by their ignorance. There is an amusing instance of the kind related in Blainville's *Travels*. A wealthy merchant, who prided himself not a little on his rare tulips, received upon one occasion a very valuable consignment of merchandise from the Levant. Intelligence of its arrival was brought him by a sailor, who presented himself for that purpose at the counting-house, among bales of goods of every description. The merchant, to reward him for his news, munificently made him a present of a fine red herring for his breakfast. The sailor had, it appears, a great partiality for onions, and seeing a bulb very like an onion lying upon the counter of this liberal trader, and thinking it, no doubt, very much out of its place among silks and velvets, he slily seized an opportunity and slipped it into his pocket, as a relish for his herring. He got clear off with his prize, and proceeded to the quay to eat his breakfast. Hardly was his back turned when the merchant missed his valuable *Semper Augustus*, worth three thousand florins, or about 280*l.* sterling. The whole establishment was instantly in an uproar; search was everywhere made for the precious root, but it was not to be found. Great was the merchant's distress of mind. The search was renewed, but again without success. At last some one thought of the sailor.

The unhappy merchant sprang into the street at the bare suggestion. His alarmed household followed him. The sailor, simple soul! had not thought of concealment. He was found quietly sitting on a coil of ropes, masticating the last morsel of his *"onion."* Little did he dream that he had been eating a breakfast whose cost might have regaled a whole ship's crew for a twelvemonth; or, as the plundered merchant himself expressed it, "might have sumptuously feasted the Prince of Orange and the whole court of the Stadtholder." Anthony caused pearls to be dissolved in wine to drink the health of Cleopatra; Sir Richard Whittington was as foolishly magnificent in an entertainment to King Henry V.; and Sir Thomas Gresham drank a diamond dissolved in wine to the health of Queen Elizabeth, when she opened the Royal Exchange; but the breakfast of this roguish Dutchman was as splendid as either. He had an advantage, too, over his wasteful predecessors: *their* gems did not improve the taste or the wholesomeness of *their* wine, while *his* tulip was quite delicious with his red herring. The most unfortunate part of the business for him was, that he remained in prison for some months on a charge of felony preferred against him by the merchant.

Another story is told of an English traveller, which is scarcely less ludicrous. This gentleman, an amateur botanist, happened to see a tulip-root lying in the conservatory of a wealthy Dutchman. Being ignorant of its quality, he took out his penknife, and peeled off its coats, with the view of making experiments upon it. When it was by this means reduced to half its size, he cut it into two equal sections, making all the time many learned remarks on the singular appearances of the unknown bulb. Suddenly the owner pounced upon him, and, with fury in his eyes, asked him if he knew what he had been doing? "Peeling a most extraordinary onion," replied the philosopher. *"Hundert tausend duyvel!"* said the Dutchman; "it's an *Admiral Van der Eyck*." "Thank you," replied the traveller, taking out his note-book to make a memorandum of the same; "are these admirals common in your country?" "Death and the Devil!" said the Dutchman, seizing the astonished man of science by the collar; "come before the syndic, and you shall see." In spite of his remonstrances, the traveller was led through the streets followed by a mob of persons. When brought into the presence of the magistrate, he learned, to his consternation, that the root upon which he had been experimentalising was worth four thousand florins; and, notwithstanding all he could urge in extenuation, he was lodged in prison until he found securities for the payment of this sum.

The demand for tulips of a rare species increased so much in the year 1636, that regular marts for their sale were established on the Stock Exchange of Amsterdam, in Rotterdam, Harlaem, Leyden, Alkmar, Hoorn, and other towns. Symptoms of gambling now became, for the first time, apparent. The stock-jobbers, ever on the alert for a new speculation, dealt largely in tulips, making use of all the means they so well knew how to employ to cause fluctuations in prices. At first, as in all these gambling mania, confidence was at its height, and every body gained. The tulip-jobbers speculated in the rise and fall of the tulip stocks, and made large profits by buying when prices fell, and selling out when they rose. Many individuals grew suddenly rich. A golden bait hung temptingly out before the people, and one after the other, they rushed to the tulip-marts, like flies around a honey-pot. Every one imagined that the passion for tulips would last for ever, and that the wealthy from every part of the world would send to Holland, and pay whatever prices were asked for them. The riches of Europe would be concentrated on the shores of the Zuyder Zee, and poverty banished from the favoured clime of Holland. Nobles, citizens, farmers, mechanics, sea-men, footmen, maid-servants, even chimney-sweeps and old clotheswomen, dabbled in tulips. People of all grades con-verted their property into cash, and invested it in flowers. Houses and lands were offered for sale at ruinously low prices, or assigned in payment of bargains made at the tulip-mart. Foreigners became smitten with the same frenzy, and money poured into Holland from all directions. The prices of the necessaries of life rose again by degrees: houses and lands, horses and carriages, and luxuries of every sort, rose in value with them, and for some months Holland seemed the very antechamber of Plutus. The operations of the trade became so extensive and so intricate, that it was found necessary to draw up a code of laws for the guidance of the dealers. Notaries and clerks were also appointed, who devoted them-selves exclusively to the interests of the trade. The designa-tion of public notary was hardly known in some towns, that of tulip-notary usurping its place. In the smaller towns, where there was no exchange, the principal tavern was usually selected as the "show-place," where high and low traded in tulips, and confirmed their bargains over sumptuous entertain-ments. These dinners were sometimes attended by two or three hundred persons, and large vases of tulips, in full bloom, were placed at regular intervals upon the tables and side-boards for their gratification during the repast.

At last, however, the more prudent began to see that this folly could not last for ever. Rich people no longer bought the flowers to keep them in their gardens, but to sell them again at cent per cent profit. It was seen that somebody must lose fearfully in the end. As this conviction spread, prices fell, and never rose again. Confidence was destroyed, and a universal panic seized upon the dealers. *A* had agreed to purchase ten *Semper Augustines* from *B*, at four thousand florins each, at six weeks after the signing of the contract. *B* was ready with the flowers at the appointed time; but the price had fallen to three or four hundred florins, and *A* refused either to pay the difference or receive the tulips. Defaulters were announced day after day in all the towns of Holland. Hundreds who, a few months previously, had begun to doubt that there was such a thing as poverty in the land suddenly found themselves the possessors of a few bulbs, which nobody would buy, even though they offered them at one quarter of the sums they had paid for them. The cry of distress resounded every where, and each man accused his neighbour. The few who had contrived to enrich themselves hid their wealth from the knowledge of their fellow-citizens, and invested it in the English or other funds. Many who, for a brief season, had emerged from the humbler walks of life, were cast back into their original obscurity. Substantial merchants were reduced almost to beggary, and many a representative of a noble line saw the fortunes of his house ruined beyond redemption.

When the first alarm subsided, the tulip-holders in the several towns held public meetings to devise what measures were best to be taken to restore public credit. It was generally agreed that deputies should be sent from all parts to Amsterdam, to consult with the government upon some remedy for the evil. The government at first refused to interfere, but advised the tulip-holders to agree to some plan among themselves. Several meetings were held for this purpose; but no measure could be devised likely to give satisfaction to the deluded people, or repair even a slight portion of the mischief that had been done. The language of complaint and reproach was in every body's mouth, and all the meetings were of the most stormy character. At last, however, after much bickering and ill-will, it was agreed, at Amsterdam, by the assembled deputies, that all contracts made in the height of the mania, or prior to the month of November, 1636, should be declared null and void, and that, in those made after that date, purchasers should be freed from their engagements, on paying ten per cent to the vendor. This decision gave no satisfaction. The vendors who had their tulips on hand were, of course, discontented, and those who had pledged themselves to purchase, thought themselves hardly treated. Tulips which had, at one time, been worth six thousand florins, were now to be procured for five hundred; so that the composition of ten per cent was one hundred florins more than the actual value. Actions for breach of contract were threatened in all the courts of the country; but the latter refused to take cognisance of gambling transactions.

The matter was finally referred to the Provincial Council at the Hague, and it was confidently expected that the wisdom of this body would invent some measure by which credit should be restored. Expectation was on the stretch for its decision, but it never came. The members continued to deliberate week after week, and at last, after thinking about it for three months, declared that they could offer no final decision until they had more information. They advised, however, that, in the meantime, every vendor should, in the presence of witnesses, offer the tulips *in natura* to the purchaser for the sums agreed upon. If the latter refused to take them, they might be put up for sale by public auction, and the original contractor held responsible for the difference between the actual and the stipulated price. This was exactly the plan recommended by the deputies, and which was already shown to be of no avail. There was no court in Holland which would enforce payment. The question was raised in Amsterdam, but the judges unanimously refused to interfere, on the ground that debts contracted in gambling were no debts in law.

Thus the matter rested. To find a remedy was beyond the power of the government. Those who were unlucky enough to have had stores of tulips on hand at the time of the sudden reaction were left to bear their ruin as philosophically as they could; those who had made profits were allowed to keep them; but the commerce of the country suffered a severe shock, from which it was many years ere it recovered.

The example of the Dutch was imitated to some extent in England. In the year 1636 tulips were publicly sold in the Exchange of London, and the jobbers exerted themselves to the utmost to raise them to the fictitious value they had acquired in Amsterdam. In Paris also the jobbers strove to create a tulipomania. In both cities they only partially succeeded. However, the force of example brought the flowers into great favour, and amongst a certain class of people tulips have ever since been prized more highly than any other flowers of the field. The Dutch are still notorious for their partiality to them, and continue to pay higher prices for them than any other people. As the rich Englishman boasts of his fine race-horses or his old pictures, so does the wealthy Dutchman vaunt him of his tulips.

In England, in our day, strange as it may appear, a tulip will produce more money than an oak. If one could be found, *rara in terris,* and black as the black swan of Juvenal, its price would equal that of a dozen acres of standing corn. In Scotland, towards the close of the seventeenth century, the highest price for tulips, according to the authority of a writer in the supplement to the third edition of the *Encyclopedia Britannica,* was ten guineas. Their value appears to have diminished from that time till the year 1769, when the two most valuable species in England were the *Don Quevedo* and the *Valentinier,* the former of which was worth two guineas and the latter two guineas and a half. These prices appear to have been the minimum. In the year 1800, a common price was fifteen guineas for a single bulb. In 1835, a bulb of the species called the Miss Fanny Kemble was sold by public auction in London for seventy-five pounds. Still more remarkable was the price of a tulip in the possession of a gardener in the King's Road, Chelsea;—in his catalogues it was labelled at two hundred guineas.